THE NEW BASICS

ELLEN LUPTON AND JENNIFER COLE PHILLIPS

Princeton Architectural Press, New York and

Maryland Institute College of Art, Baltimore

Published by
Princeton Architectural Press
37 East Seventh Street
New York, New York 10003

For a free catalog of books, call
1.800.722.6657.
Visit our website at www.papress.com.

Library of Congress Cataloging-in-Publication Data
Lupton, Ellen.
  Graphic design : the new basics / Ellen Lupton and
Jennifer Cole Phillips.
      247 p. : ill. (chiefly col.) ; 23 cm.
Includes bibliographical references and index.
ISBN 978-1-56898-770-5 (hardcover : alk. paper)
ISBN 978-1-56898-702-6 (paperback : alk. paper)
1. Graphic arts. I. Phillips, Jennifer C., 1960– II. Title.
NC997.L87 2008
741.6—dc22
                                        2007033805

For Maryland Institute College of Art

Book Design
Ellen Lupton and Jennifer Cole Phillips

Contributing Faculty
Ken Barber
Kimberly Bost
Jeremy Botts
Corinne Botz
Bernard Canniffe
Nancy Froehlich
Ellen Lupton
Al Maskeroni
Ryan McCabe
Abbott Miller
Jennifer Cole Phillips
James Ravel
Zvezdana Rogic
Nolen Strals
Mike Weikert
Bruce Willen
Yeohyun Ahn

Visiting Artists
Marian Bantjes
Nicholas Blechman
Alicia Cheng
Peter Cho
Malcolm Grear
David Plunkert
C. E. B. Reas
Paul Sahre
Jan van Toorn
Rick Valicenti

For Princeton Architectural Press

Editor
Clare Jacobson

Special thanks to
Nettie Aljian, Sara Bader, Dorothy Ball,
Nicola Bednarek, Janet Behning, Becca Casbon,
Penny (Yuen Pik) Chu, Russell Fernandez,
Pete Fitzpatrick, Wendy Fuller, Jan Haux,
Aileen Kwun, Nancy Eklund Later, Linda
Lee, Laurie Manfra, Katharine Myers, Lauren
Nelson Packard, Jennifer Thompson, Arnoud
Verhaeghe, Paul Wagner, Joseph Weston, and
Deb Wood — *Kevin C. Lippert, publisher*

Contents

Foreword

Ellen Lupton and Jennifer Cole Phillips

How do designers get ideas? Some places they look are design annuals and monographs, searching for clever combinations of forms, fonts, and colors to inspire their projects. For students and professionals who want to dig deeper into how form works, this book shows how to build richness and complexity around simple relationships. We created this book because we didn't see anything like it available for today's students and young designers: a concise, visually inspiring guide to two-dimensional design.

As educators with decades of combined experience in graduate and undergraduate teaching, we have witnessed the design world change and change again in response to new technologies. When we were students ourselves in the 1980s, classic books such as Armin Hofmann's *Graphic Design Manual* (published in 1965) had begun to lose their relevance within the restless and shifting design scene. Postmodernism was on the rise, and abstract design exercises seemed out of step with the current interest in appropriation and historicism.

During the 1990s, design educators became caught in the pressure to teach (and learn) software, and many of us struggled to balance technical skills with visual and critical thinking. Form sometimes got lost along the way, as design methodologies moved away from universal visual concepts toward a more anthropological understanding of design as a constantly changing flow of cultural sensibilities.

This book addresses the gap between software and visual thinking. By focusing on form, we have re-embraced the Bauhaus tradition and the pioneering work of the great formal design educators, from Armin Hofmann to some of our own teachers, including Malcolm Grear. We believe that a common ground of visual principles connects designers across history and around the globe.

We initiated this project in 2005, after stepping back and noticing that our students were not at ease building concepts abstractly. Although they were adept at working and reworking pop-culture vocabularies, they were less comfortable manipulating scale, rhythm, color, hierarchy, grids, and diagrammatic relationships.

In this book, you won't see exercises or demonstrations involving parody or cultural critique—not that there is anything wrong with those lines of inquiry. Designers and educators will always build personal meaning and social content into their work. With this book we chose to focus, however, on design's formal structures.

This is a book for students and emerging designers, and it is illustrated primarily with student work, produced within graduate and undergraduate design studios. Our school, Maryland Institute College of Art (MICA), became our laboratory. Numerous faculty and scores of students participated in our brave experiment over a two-year period. The work that emerged is varied and diverse, reflecting an organic range of skill levels and sensibilities. Unless otherwise noted, all the student examples were generated in the context of MICA's courses; a few projects originate from schools we visited or where our own graduate students are teaching.

Our student contributors come from China, India, Japan, Korea, Puerto Rico, Trinidad, Seattle, Minneapolis, Baltimore, rural Pennsylvania, and many other places. The book was manufactured in China and published with Princeton Architectural Press in New York City.

This book was thus created in a global context. The work presented within its pages is energized by the diverse backgrounds of its producers, whose creativity is shaped by their cultural identities as well as by their unique life experiences. A common thread that draws all these people together in one place is design.

The majority of student work featured here comes from the course we teach together at MICA, the Graphic Design MFA Studio. Our MFA program's first publishing venture was the book *D.I.Y.: Design It Yourself* (2006), directed at general readers who want to use design in their own lives. Currently underway is a guide to independent publishing, along with other titles devoted to expanding access to and the understanding of design processes.

The current volume, *Graphic Design: The New Basics*, marks the launch of MICA's Center for Design Thinking, an umbrella for organizing the college's diverse efforts in the area of practical design research. In addition to publishing books about design, the Center for Design Thinking will organize conferences and educational events to help build the design discourse while creating invaluable opportunities for MICA's students and faculty.

To complement the student work featured in this project, we have selected key examples from contemporary professional practice. These works demonstrate experimental, visually rich design approaches conducted at the highest possible level.

Many of the designers featured, including Marian Bantjes, Alicia Cheng, Peter Cho, Malcolm Grear, David Plunkert, C. E. B. Reas, Paul Sahre, Rick Valicenti, and Jan van Toorn, have worked with our students as visiting artists at MICA. Some conducted special workshops whose results are included in this volume.

Graphic Design: The New Basics lays out the elements of a visual language whose forms are employed by individuals, institutions, and locales that are increasingly connected in a global society. We hope the book will inspire more thought and creativity.

Acknowledgments

My work creating this book constituted my degree project in the Doctorate in Communication Design program at the University of Baltimore. I thank my advisors, Stuart Moulthrop, Sean Carton, and Amy Pointer. I also thank my colleagues at MICA, including Fred Lazarus, President; Ray Allen, Provost; Leslie King Hammond, Dean of Graduate Studies; and my longtime friend and collaborator, Jennifer Cole Phillips. Special thanks go to the dozens of students whose work enlivens these pages.

Editor Clare Jacobson and the team at Princeton Architectural Press helped make the book real.

My whole family is an inspiration, especially my parents Bill, Shirley, Mary Jane, and Ken; my children Jay and Ruby; my sisters Julia and Michelle; and my husband Abbott.

Ellen Lupton

My contribution to this book is dedicated to Malcolm Grear, my lifelong mentor and friend.

The culture at MICA is a joy in which to work, thanks in large part to the vision and support of Fred Lazarus, President; Ray Allen, Provost; and Leslie King Hammond, Dean of Graduate Studies; and our savvy and talented faculty colleagues. Many thanks to our student contributors, especially the Graphic Design MFA group; this book exudes their energy. I hold heartfelt gratitude for my friend and close collaborator, Ellen Lupton, for her generosity and grace.

Clare Jacobson and Wendy Fuller at Princeton Architectural Press were invaluable with their expertise.

My family, especially my parents Ann and Jack and my sisters Lanie and Jodie, are a constant source of encouragement and support.

Jennifer Cole Phillips

Back to the Bauhaus

Ellen Lupton

The idea of searching out a shared framework in which to invent and organize visual content dates back to the origins of modern graphic design. In the 1920s, institutions such as the Bauhaus in Germany explored design as a universal, perceptually based "language of vision," a concept that continues to shape design education today around the world.

This book reflects on that vital tradition in light of profound shifts in technology and global social life. Whereas the Bauhaus promoted rational solutions through planning and standardization, designers and artists today are drawn to idiosyncrasy, customization, and sublime accidents as well as to standards and norms. The modernist preference for reduced, simplified forms now coexists with a desire to build systems that yield unexpected results. Today, the impure, the contaminated, and the hybrid hold as much allure as forms that are sleek and perfected. Visual thinkers often seek to spin out intricate results from simple rules or concepts rather than reduce an image or idea to its simplest parts.

The Bauhaus Legacy In the 1920s, faculty at the Bauhaus and other schools analyzed form in terms of basic geometric elements. They believed this language would be understandable to everyone, grounded in the universal instrument of the eye.

Bauhaus faculty pursued this idea from different points of view. Wassily Kandinsky called for the creation of a "dictionary of elements" and a universal visual "grammar" in his Bauhaus textbook *Point and Line to Plane*. His colleague László Moholy-Nagy sought to uncover a rational vocabulary ratified by a shared society and a common humanity. Courses taught by Josef Albers emphasized systematic thinking over personal intuition, objectivity over emotion.

Albers and Moholy-Nagy forged the use of new media and new materials. They saw that art and design were being transformed by technology—photography, film, and mass production. And yet their ideas remained profoundly humanistic, always asserting the role of the individual over the absolute authority of any system or method. Design, they argued, is never reducible to its function or to a technical description.

Since the 1940s, numerous educators have refined and expanded on the Bauhaus approach, from Moholy-Nagy and Gyorgy Kepes at the New Bauhaus in Chicago; to Johannes Itten, Max Bill, and Gui Bonsiepe at the Ulm School in Germany; to Emil Ruder and Armin Hofmann in Switzerland; to the "new typographies" of Wolfgang Weingart, Dan Friedman, and Katherine McCoy in Switzerland and the United States. Each of these revolutionary educators articulated structural approaches to design from distinct and original perspectives.

Some of them also engaged in the postmodern rejection of universal communication. According to postmodernism, which emerged in the 1960s, it is futile to look for inherent meaning in an image or object because people will bring their own cultural biases and personal experiences to the process of interpretation. As postmodernism itself became a dominant ideology in the 1980s and '90s, in both the academy and in the marketplace, the design process got mired in the act of referencing cultural styles or tailoring messages to narrowly defined communities.

The New Basics Designers at the Bauhaus believed not only in a universal way of *describing* visual form, but also in its universal *significance*. Reacting against that belief, postmodernism discredited formal experiment as a primary component of thinking and making in the visual arts. Formal study was considered to be tainted by its link to universalistic ideologies. This book recognizes a difference between description and interpretation, between a potentially universal language of making and the universality of meaning.

Today, software designers have realized the Bauhaus goal of describing (but not interpreting) the language of vision in a universal way. Software organizes visual material into menus of properties, parameters, filters, and so on, creating tools that are universal in their social ubiquity, cross-disciplinarity, and descriptive power. Photoshop, for example, is a systematic study of the features of an image (its contrast, size, color model, and so on). InDesign and QuarkXpress are structural explorations of typography: they are software machines for controlling leading, alignment, spacing, and column structures as well as image placement and page layout.

In the aftermath of the Bauhaus, textbooks of basic design have returned again and again to elements such as point, line, plane, texture, and color, organized by principles of scale, contrast, movement, rhythm, and balance. This book revisits those concepts as well as looking at some of the new universals emerging today.

Transparency and Layers The Google Earth interface allows users to manipulate the transparency of overlays placed over satellite photographs of Earth. Here, Hurricane Katrina hovers over the Gulf Coast of the U.S. Storm: University of Wisconsin, Madison Cooperative Institute for Meteorogical Satellite Studies, 2005. Composite: Jack Gondela.

What are these emerging universals? What is new in basic design? Consider, for example, transparency—a concept explored in this book. Transparency is a condition in which two or more surfaces or substances are visible through each other. We constantly experience transparency in the physical environment: from water, glass, and smoke to venetian blinds, slatted fences, and perforated screens. Graphic designers across the modern period have worked with transparency, but never more so than today, when transparency can be instantly manipulated with commonly used tools.

What does transparency *mean*? Transparency can be used to construct thematic relationships. For example, compressing two pictures into a single space can suggest a conflict or synthesis of ideas (East/West, male/female, old/new). Designers also employ transparency as a compositional (rather than thematic) device, using it to soften edges, establish emphasis, separate competing elements, and so on.

Transparency is crucial to the vocabulary of film and motion-based media. In place of a straight cut, an animator or editor diminishes the opacity of an image over time (fade to black) or mixes two semitransparent images (cross dissolve). Such transitions affect a film's rhythm and style. They also modulate, in subtle ways, the message or content of the work. Although viewers rarely stop to interpret these transitions, a video editor or animator understands them as part of the basic language of moving images.

Layering is another universal concept with rising importance. Physical printing processes use layers (ink on paper), and so do software interfaces (from layered Photoshop files to sound or motion timelines).

Transparency and layering have always been at play in the graphic arts. In today's context, what makes them new again is their omnipresent accessibility through software. Powerful digital tools are commonly available to professional artists and designers but also to children, amateurs, and tinkerers of every stripe. Their language has become universal.

Software tools provide models of visual media, but they don't tell us what to make or what to say. It is the designer's task to produce works that are relevant to living situations (audience, context, program, brief, site) and to deliver meaningful messages and rich, embodied experiences. Each producer animates design's core structures from his or her own place in the world.

Beyond the Basics

Jennifer Cole Phillips

Even the most robust visual language is useless without the ability to engage it in a living context. While this book centers around formal structure and experiment, some opening thoughts on process and problem solving are appropriate here, as we hope readers will reach not only for more accomplished form, but for form that resonates with fresh meaning.

Before the Macintosh, solving graphic design problems meant outsourcing at nearly every stage of the way: manuscripts were sent to a typesetter; photographs—selected from contact sheets—were printed at a lab and corrected by a retoucher; and finished artwork was the job of a paste-up artist, who sliced and cemented type and images onto boards. This protocol slowed down the work process and required designers to plan each step methodically.

By contrast, powerful, off-the-shelf software now allows designers and users of all ilks to endlessly edit their work in the comfort of a personal or professional workspace.

Yet, as these digital technologies afford greater freedom and convenience, they also require ongoing education and upkeep. This recurring learning curve, added to already overloaded schedules, often cuts short the creative window for concept development and formal experimentation.

In the college context, students arrive ever more digitally facile. Acculturated by iPods, Playstations, and PowerBooks, design students command the technical savvy that used to take years to build. Being plugged in, however, has not always profited creative thinking.

Too often, the temptation to turn directly to the computer precludes deeper levels of research and ideation—the distillation zone that unfolds beyond the average appetite for testing the waters and exploring alternatives. People, places, thoughts, and things become familiar through repeated exposure. It stands to reason, then, that initial ideas and, typically, the top tiers of a Google search turn up only cursory results that are often tired and trite.

Getting to more interesting territory requires the perseverance to sift, sort, and assimilate subjects and solutions until a fresh spark emerges and takes hold.

Visual Thinking Ubiquitous access to image editing and design software, together with zealous media inculcation on all things design, has created a tidal wave of design makers outside our profession. Indeed, in our previous book, *D.I.Y.: Design It Yourself*, we extolled the virtues of learning and making, arguing that people acquire pleasure, knowledge, and power by engaging with design at all levels.

With this volume we shift the climate of the conversation. Instead of skimming the surface, we dig deeper. Rather than issuing instructions, we frame problems and suggest possibilities. Inside, you will find many examples, by students and professionals, that balance and blend idiosyncrasy with formal discipline.

Rather than focus on practical problems such as how to design a book, brochure, logo, or website, this book encourages readers to experiment with the visual language of design. By "experiment," we mean the process of examining a form, material, or process in a methodical yet open-ended way. To experiment is to isolate elements of an operation, limiting some variables in order to better study others. An experiment asks a question or tests a hypothesis whose answer is not known in advance.

Choose your corner, pick away at it carefully, intensely and to the best of your ability and that way **you might change the world.** Charles Eames

The book is organized around some of the formal elements and phenomena of design. In practice, those components mix and overlap, as they do in the examples shown throughout the book. By focusing attention on particular aspects of visual form, we encourage readers to recognize the forces at play behind strong graphic solutions. Likewise, while a dictionary studies specific words in isolation, those words come alive in the active context of writing and speaking.

Filtered through formal and conceptual experimentation, design thinking fuses a shared discipline with organic interpretation.

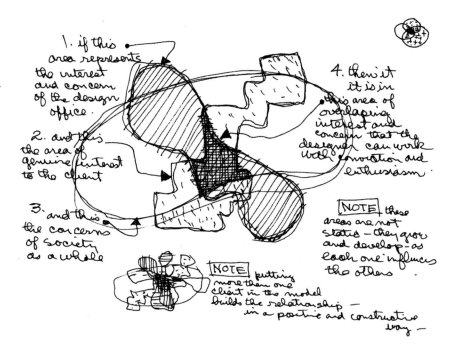

Diagramming Process Charles Eames drew this diagram to explain the design process as achieving a point where the needs and interests of the client, the designer, and society as a whole overlap. Charles Eames, 1969, for the exhibition "What is Design" at the Musée des Arts décoratifs, Paris, France. © 2007 Eames Office LLC.

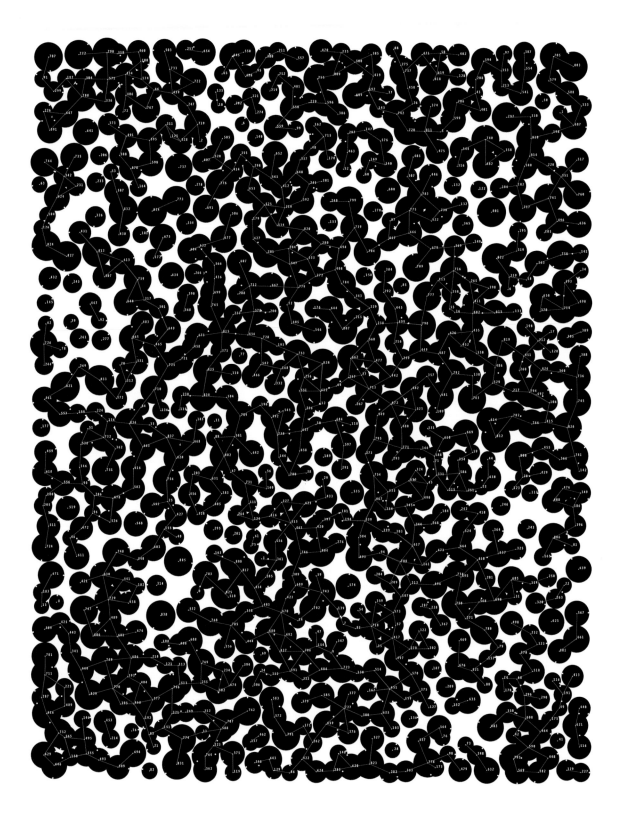

Point, Line, Plane

A line is the track made by the moving point...
It is created by movement—specifically through
the destruction of the intense, self-contained
repose of the point. Wassily Kandinsky

Id	0	1	2	3
X	224.543	715.448	227.491	313.495
Y	247.001	879.651	839.485	291.144
Size	20.000	20.024	20.048	20.072
Angle	1.429	1.000	4.141	0.144
Others	2	1	2	1
	29	30	31	32	33
	396.477	386.946	655.302	347.761	158.650
	396.899	468.870	242.406	625.749	466.553
	20.691	20.715	20.739	20.763	20.787
	4.687	5.715	5.395	3.691	6.245
	1	3	2	2	2
	59	60	61	62	63
	388.065	450.679	302.301	18.621	9.702
	269.422	795.973	319.802	598.880	782.143
	21.406	21.430	21.454	21.478	21.502
	2.471	2.117	1.626	0.988	3.603
	1	1	2	1	2
	89	90	91	92	93
	247.620	67.441	13.802	90.058	440.551
	450.361	388.695	920.408	602.967	200.302
	22.122	22.145	22.169	22.193	22.217
	2.354	0.952	2.805	0.112	2.384
	4	3	2	1	2

Point to Line Processing is a programming
language created by C. E. B. Reas and
Benjamin Fry. In this digital drawing by Reas,
the lines express a relationship among the
points, derived from numerical data. C. E. B.
Reas. *Process 4 (Form/Data 1)*, 2005 (detail).

Point, line, and plane are the building blocks of design. From these elements, designers create images, icons, textures, patterns, diagrams, animations, and typographic systems. Indeed, every complex design shown in this book results at some level from the interaction of points, lines, and planes.

Diagrams build relationships among elements using points, lines, and planes to map and connect data. Textures and patterns are constructed from large groups of points and lines that repeat, rotate, and otherwise interact to form distinctive and engaging surfaces. Typography consists of individual letters (points) that form into lines and fields of text.

For hundreds of years, printing processes have employed dots and lines to depict light, shadow, and volume. Different printing technologies support distinct kinds of mark making. To produce a woodcut, for example, the artist carves out material from a flat surface. In contrast to this subtractive process, lithography allows the artist to make positive, additive marks across a surface. In these processes, dots and lines accumulate to build larger planes and convey the illusion of volume.

Photography, invented in the early 1800s, captures reflected light automatically. The subtle tonal variations of photography eliminated the intermediary mesh of point and line.

Yet reproducing the tones of a photographic image requires translating it into pure graphic marks, because nearly every mechanical printing method—from lithography to laser printing—works with solid inks. The halftone process, invented in the 1880s and still used today, converts a photograph into a pattern of larger and smaller dots, simulating tonal variation with pure spots of black or flat color. The same principle is used in digital reproduction.

Today, designers use software to capture the gestures of the hand as data that can be endlessly manipulated and refined. Software describes images in terms of point, line, plane, shape, and volume as well as color, transparency, and other features. There are numerous ways to experiment with these basic elements of two-dimensional design: observing the environment around you, making marks with physical and digital tools, using software to create and manipulate images, or writing code to generate form with rules and variables.

$x = 4.5521$ in
$y = 0.997$ in

Point

A point marks a position in space. In pure geometric terms, a point is a pair of x, y coordinates. It has no mass at all. Graphically, however, a point takes form as a dot, a visible mark. A point can be an insignificant fleck of matter or a concentrated locus of power. It can penetrate like a bullet, pierce like a nail, or pucker like a kiss. Through its scale, position, and relationship to its surroundings, a point can express its own identity or melt into the crowd.

A series of points forms a line. A mass of points becomes texture, shape, or plane. Tiny points of varying size create shades of gray.

The tip of an arrow points the way, just as the crossing of an X marks a spot.

In typography, the point is a period—the definitive end of a line. Each character in a field of text is a singular element, and thus a kind of point, a finite element in a series.

end of a line.

In typography, each character in a field of text is a point, a finite element represented by a single key stroke. The letter occupies a position in a larger line or plane of text. At the end of the line is a period. The point is a sign of closure, of finality. It marks the end.

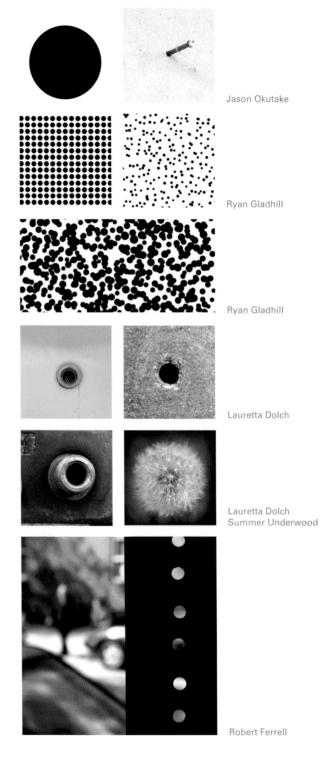

Jason Okutake

Ryan Gladhill

Ryan Gladhill

Lauretta Dolch

Lauretta Dolch
Summer Underwood

Robert Ferrell

Digital Imaging. Al Maskeroni, faculty.

Destructive Points Never underestimate
the power of a point. This damaged facade
was photographed in the war-torn city of
Mostar, on the Balkan Peninsula in Bosnia
and Herzegovina. Nancy Froehlich.

Jeremy Botts

Lines express emotions.

length = .9792 in

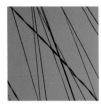
Josh Sims
Bryan McDonough

Alex Ebright
Justin Lloyd

Digital Imaging.
Nancy Froehlich,
faculty.

Lines describe structure and edges.

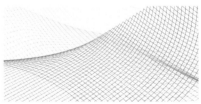
Allen Harrison

Lines turn and multiply to describe planes.

Line

A line is an infinite series of points. Understood geometrically, a line has length, but no breadth. A line is the connection between two points, or it is the path of a moving point.

A line can be a positive mark or a negative gap. Lines appear at the edges of objects and where two planes meet.

Graphically, lines exist in many weights; the thickness and texture as well as the path of the mark determine its visual presence. Lines are drawn with a pen, pencil, brush, mouse, or digital code. They can be straight or curved, continuous or broken. When a line reaches a certain thickness, it becomes a plane. Lines multiply to describe volumes, planes, and textures.

A graph is a rising and falling line that describes change over time, as in a waveform charting a heart beat or an audio signal.

In typographic layouts, lines are implied as well as literally drawn. Characters group into lines of text, while columns are positioned in blocks that are flush left, flush right, and justified. Imaginary lines appear along the edges of each column, expressing the order of the page.

Type sits on a baseline.

Typographic alignment refers to the organization of text into columns with a hard or soft edge. A justified column is even along both the left and right sides.

The crisp edge of a column is implied by the even starting or ending points of successive lines of type. The eye connects the points to make a line. Such typographic lines are implied, not drawn.

Line/Shape Study Vector-based software uses a closed line to define a shape. Here, new lines are formed by the intersection of shapes, creating a swelling form reminiscent of the path of a steel-point pen. Ryan Gladhill, MFA Studio.

width = 0.9792 in
height = 0.9792 in

Plane

A plane is a flat surface extending in height and width. A plane is the path of a moving line; it is a line with breadth. A line closes to become a shape, a bounded plane. Shapes are planes with edges. In vector-based software, every shape consists of line and fill. A plane can be parallel to the picture surface, or it can skew and recede into space. Ceilings, walls, floors, and windows are physical planes. A plane can be solid or perforated, opaque or transparent, textured or smooth.

A field of text is a plane built from points and lines of type. A typographic plane can be dense or open, hard or soft. Designers experiment with line spacing, font size, and alignment to create different typographic shapes.

In typography, letters gather into lines, and lines build up into planes. The quality of the plane—its density or opacity, its heaviness or lightness on the page—is determined by the size of the letters, the spacing between lines, words, and characters, and the visual character of a given typeface.

In typography, letters gather into lines, and lines build up into planes. The quality of the plane—its density, its opacity, its weight on the page—is determined by the size of the letters, the spacing between lines, words, and characters, and the visual character of a given typeface.

Hard, closed shape

Soft, open shape

Plane Letters A plane can be described with lines or with fields of color. These letterforms use ribbons of color to describe spatial planes. Kelly Horigan, Experimental Typography. Ken Barber, faculty.

**Parallel Lines
Converge**
Summer
Underwood

Space and Volume

A graphic object that encloses three-dimensional space has volume. It has height, width, and depth. A sheet of paper or a computer screen has no real depth, of course, so volume is represented through graphic conventions.

Linear perspective simulates optical distortions, making near objects appear large as far objects become small, receding into nothing as they reach the horizon. The angle at which elements recede reflects the position of the viewer. Are the objects above or below the viewer's eye level? Camera lenses replicate the effects of linear perspective, recording the position of the camera's eye.

Axonometric projections depict volume without making elements recede into space. The scale of elements thus remains consistent as objects move back into space. The result is more abstract and impersonal than linear perspective.

Architects often use axonometric projections in order to keep a consistent scale across the page. Digital game designers often use this technique as well, creating maps of simulated worlds rather than depicting experience from the ground.

Projection Study This idealized landscape uses axonometric projection, in which scale is consistent from the front to back of the image. As seen on a map or computer game, this space implies a disembodied, godlike viewer rather than a physical eye positioned in relation to a horizon. Visakh Menon, MFA Studio.

Yeohyun Ahn

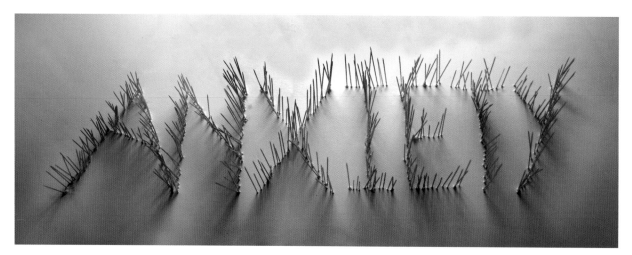

Visakh Menon

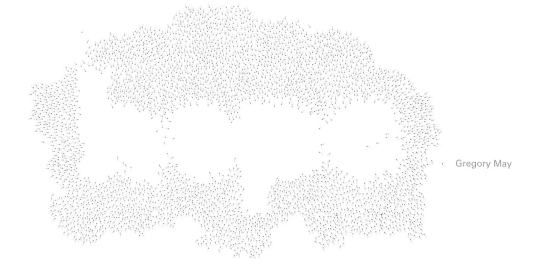

Gregory May

Yeohyun Ahn

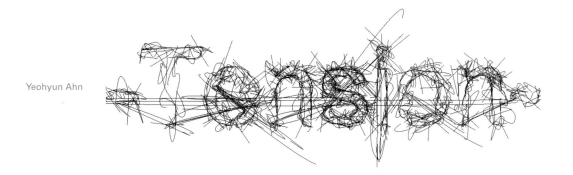

Jason Okutake

Point and Line: Physical and Digital In the lettering experiments shown here, each word is written with lines, points, or both, produced with physical elements, digital illustrations, or code-generated vectors. MFA Studio. Marian Bantjes, visiting faculty.

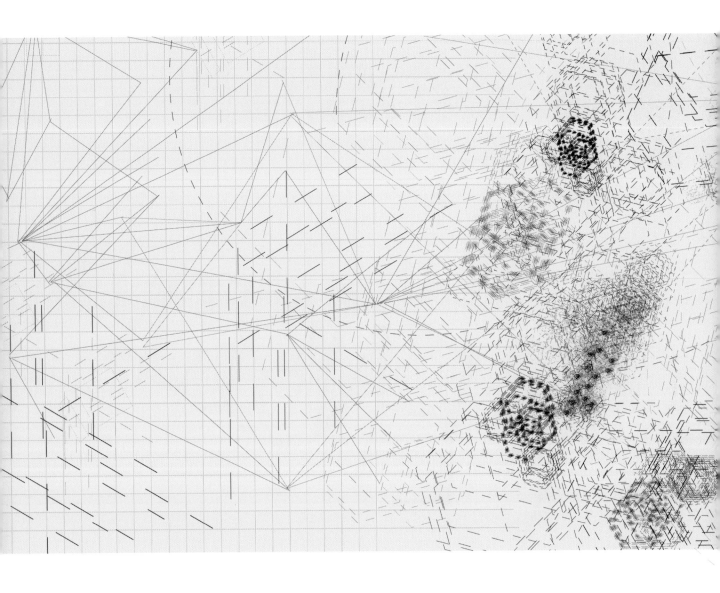

Line Study: Order and Disorder Inspired
by maps of population density, this digital
drawing uses lines to describe shapes and
volumes as well as to form dense splotches
of texture. The drawing originates from
the center with a series of hexagons. As the
hexagons migrate to the left, they become
more open. As they migrate to the right,
they erode, becoming soft and organic. Ryan
Gladhill, MFA Studio.

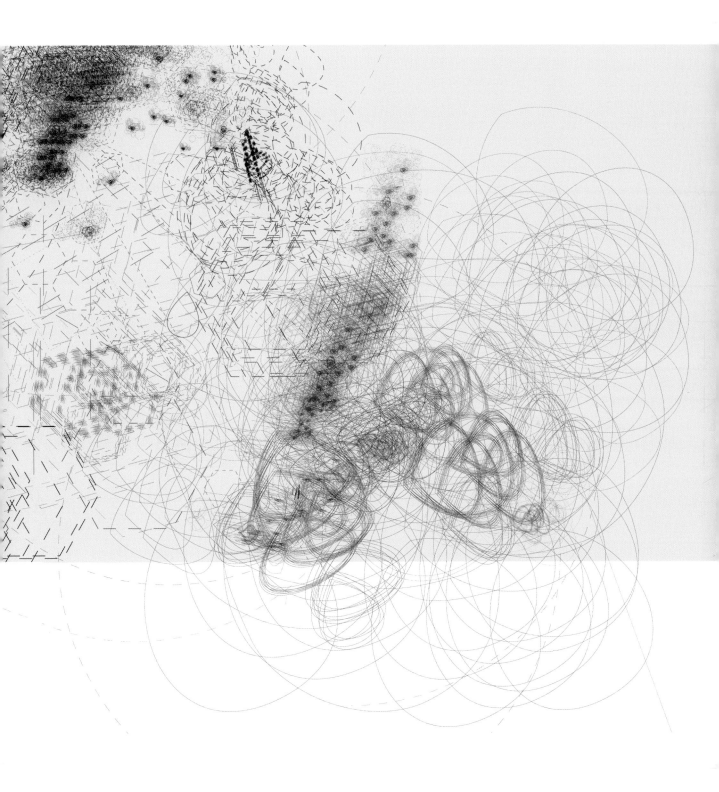

BinaryTree(400,600,400,550,30,1);

BinaryTree(400,600,400,550,30,3);

Drawing with Code

The drawings shown here were created with Processing, an open-source software application. The designs are built from a binary tree, a basic data structure in which each node spawns at most two offspring. Binary trees are used to organize information hierarchies, and they often take a graphical form. The density of the final drawing depends on the angle between the "children" and the number of generations.

The larger design is created by repeating, rotating, inverting, connecting, and overlapping the tree forms. In code-based drawing, the designer varies the results by changing the inputs to the algorithm.

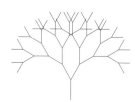

BinaryTree(400,600,400,550,30,5);

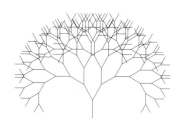

BinaryTree(400,600,400,550,30,7);

BinaryTree(400,600,400,550,30,9);

Binary Tree The drawing becomes denser with each generation. The last number in the code indicates the number of iterations. Yeohyun Ahn, MFA Studio.

Binary Tree Pattern Produced with code, this textured drawing employs techniques that have been used across history to produce rhythmic patterns: copying, repeating, rotating, inverting, and connecting. Yeohyun Ahn, MFA Studio.

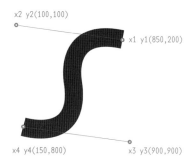

x2 y2(100,100)

x1 y1(850,200)

x4 y4(150,800)

x3 y3(900,900)

bezier(850,200,100,100,900,900,150,800);

for(int i=0; i<900; i=i+100)
{bezier(850,200,100,100,i,900,150,800);}

Bézier Curves

A Bézier curve is a line defined by a set of anchor and control points. Designers are accustomed to drawing curves using vector-based software and then modifying the curve by adding, subtracting, and repositioning the anchor and control points.

The drawings shown here were created with the open-source software application Processing. The curves were drawn directly in code:

bezier(x1,y1,x2,y2,x3,y3,x4,y4);

The first two parameters (x1, y1) specify the first anchor point, and the last two parameters (x4, y4) specify the other anchor point. The middle parameters locate the control points that define the curve.

Curves drawn with standard illustration software are fundamentally the same as curves drawn in code, but we understand and control them with different means. The designer varies the results by changing the inputs to the algorithm.

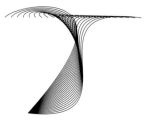

for(int i=0;i<900; i=i+40)
{bezier(i,200,100,100,900,i,150,800);}

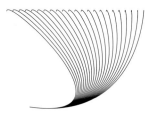

for(int i=0;i<900;i=i+40)
{bezier(i,200,i,100,900,900,150,800);}

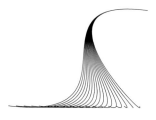

for(int i=0; i<900; i=i+50)
{bezier(900,200,100,100,900,900,i,800);}

for(int i=0; i<900; i=i+100)
{bezier(900,200,100,100,900,i,50,800);}

Repeated Bézier Curve The designer has written a function that repeats the curve in space according to a given increment (i). The same basic code was used to generate all the drawings shown above, with varied inputs for the anchor and control points. A variable (i) defines the curve. Yeohyun Ahn, MFA Studio.

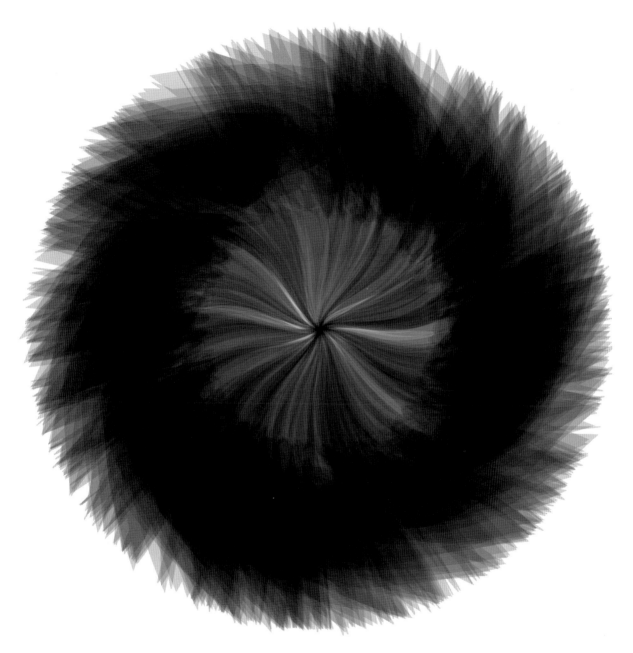

```
beginShape(POLYGON);
vertex(30,20);
bezierVertex(80,0,80,75,30,75);
bezierVertex(50,80,60,25,30,20);
endShape()
```

Black Flower A Bézier vertex is a shape
created by closing a Bézier curve. This
design was created by rotating numerous
Bézier vertices around a common center,
with varying degrees of transparency.
Yeohyun Ahn, MFA Studio.

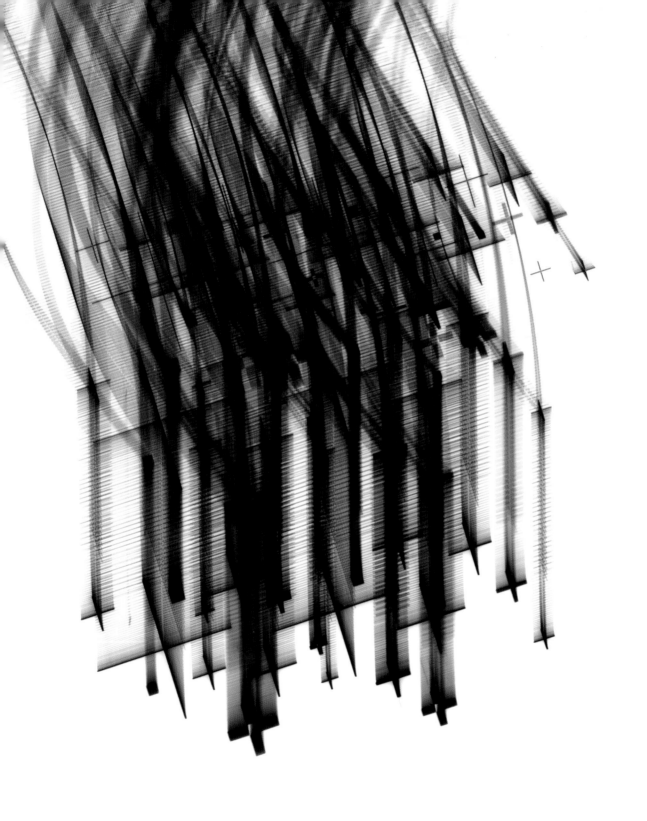

Rhythm and Balance

I pay close attention to the variety of shapes and sizes, and place the objects so that **the lines and edges create a rhythm** that guides the viewer's eye around the image and into the focal point. Sergei Forostovskii

Rhythm and Repetition This code-driven photogram employs a simple stencil plus sign through which light is projected as the photo paper shifts minutely and mechanically across the span of hours. The visual result has the densely layered richness of a charcoal drawing. Tad Takano. Photographed for reproduction by Dan Meyers.

Balance is a fundamental human condition: we require physical balance to stand upright and walk; we seek balance among the many facets of our personal and professional lives; the world struggles for balance of power. Indeed, balance is a prized commodity in our culture, and it is no surprise that our implicit, intuitive relationship with it has equipped us to sense balance—or imbalance—in the things we see, hear, smell, taste, and touch.

In design, balance acts as a catalyst for form—it anchors and activates elements in space. Do you ever notice your eye getting stuck in a particular place when looking at an unresolved design? This discord usually occurs because the proportion and placement of elements in relation to each other and to the negative space is off—too big, too tight, too flat, misaligned, and so on.

Relationships among elements on the page remind us of physical relationships. Visual balance occurs when the weight of one or more things is distributed evenly or proportionately in space. Like arranging furniture in a room, we move components around until the balance of form and space feels just right. Large objects are a counterpoint to smaller ones; dark objects to lighter ones.

A symmetrical design, which has the same elements on at least two sides along a common axis, is inherently stable. Yet balance need not be static. A tightrope walker achieves balance while traversing a precarious line in space, continually shifting her weight while staying in constant motion. Designers employ contrasting size, texture, value, color, and shape to offset or emphasize the weight of an object and achieve the acrobat's dynamic sense of balance.

Rhythm is a strong, regular, repeated pattern: the beating of drums, the patter of rain, the falling of footsteps. Speech, music, and dance all employ rhythm to express form over time. Graphic designers use rhythm in the construction of static images as well as in books, magazines, and motion graphics that have duration and sequence. Although pattern design usually employs unbroken repetition, most forms of graphic design seek rhythms that are punctuated with change and variation. Book design, for example, seeks out a variety of scales and tonal values across its pages, while also preserving an underlying structural unity.

Balance and rhythm work together to create works of design that pulse with life, achieving both stability and surprise.

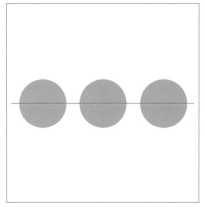
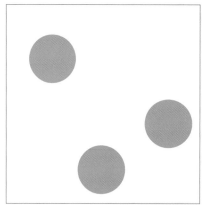
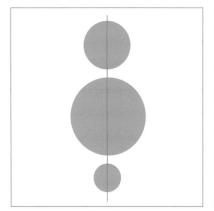

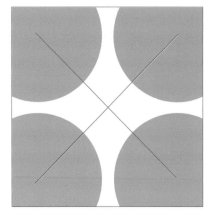

Symmetry and Asymmetry
Symmetry can be left to right, top to bottom, or both. Many natural organisms have a symmetrical form. The even weighting of arms and legs helps insure a creature's safe mobility; a tree develops an even distribution of weight around its core to stand erect; and the arms of a starfish radiate from the center.

Symmetry is not the only way to achieve balance, however. Asymmetrical designs are generally more active than symmetrical ones, and designers achieve balance by placing contrasting elements in counterpoint to each other, yielding compositions that allow the eye to wander while achieving an overall stability.

Symmetry The studies above demonstrate basic symmetrical balance. Elements are oriented along a common axis; the image mirrors from side to side along that axis. The configurations shown here are symmetrical from left to right and/or from top to bottom.

Asymmetry These studies use asymmetry to achieve compositional balance. Elements are placed organically, relying on the interaction of form and negative space and the proximity of elements to each other and to the edges of the field, yielding both tension and balance.

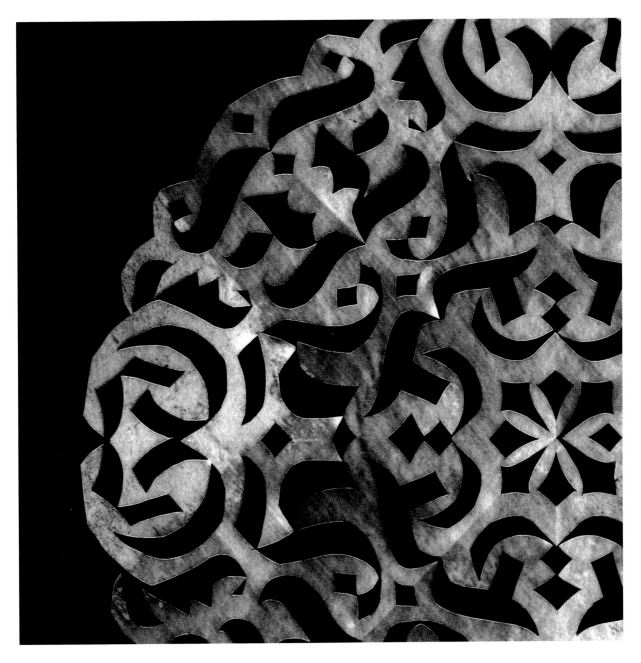

Symmetry and Asymmetry The designer
has cropped a symmetrical form in order to
create an asymmetrical composition.
A rhythm of repeated elements undulates
across the surface. The larger ornamental
form has been shifted dramatically off center,
yielding dynamic balance. Jeremy Botts,
MFA Studio.

Highway Overpasses, Houston, Texas

Shipping Containers, Norfolk, Virginia

Repetition and Change
From the flowing contours of a farmer's fields to a sea of cars tucked into the lined compartments of a parking lot, repetition is an endless feature of the human environment. Like melodic consonance and fervent discord in music, repetition and change awaken life's visual juxtapositions. Beauty arises from the mix.

Contour Farming, Meyersville, Maryland

Port of Baltimore, Maryland

Arlington National Cemetery,
Washington, D.C.

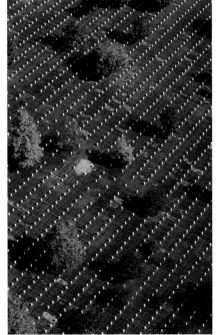

Observed Rhythm Aerial photographs are
fascinating and surprising because we
are not accustomed to seeing landscapes
from above. The many patterns, textures,
and colors embedded in both man-made
and natural forms—revealed and concealed
through light and shadow—yield intriguing
rhythms. Cameron Davidson.

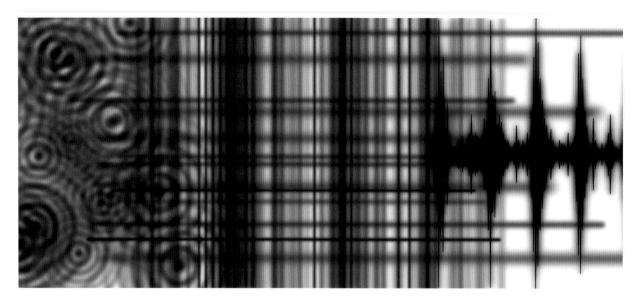

Jason Okutake, MFA Studio

Rhythm and Time

We are familiar with rhythm from the world of sound. In music, an underlying pattern changes in time. Layers of pattern occur simultaneously in music, supporting each other and providing aural contrast. In audio mixing, sounds are amplified or diminished to create a rhythm that shifts and evolves over the course of a piece.

Graphic designers employ similar structures visually. The repetition of elements such as circles, lines, and grids creates rhythm, while varying their size or intensity generates surprise. In animation, designers must orchestrate both audio and visual rhythms simultaneously.

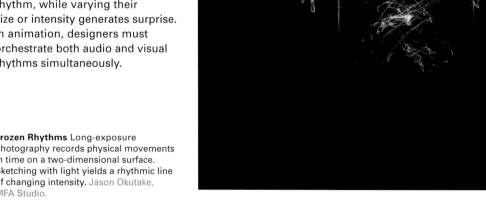

Frozen Rhythms Long-exposure photography records physical movements in time on a two-dimensional surface. Sketching with light yields a rhythmic line of changing intensity. Jason Okutake, MFA Studio.

Pattern Dissonance Letterforms with abruptly
shifting features are built around a thin
skeleton. The strange anatomy of the letters
plays against the comfortable, gentle rhythms
of the old-fashioned wallpaper behind them.
Jeremy Botts, MFA Studio.

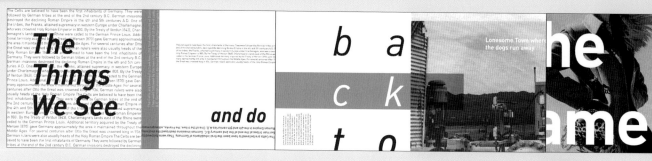

Rhythm and Pacing

Designers often work with content distributed across many pages. As in a single-page composition, a sequential design must possess an overall coherence. Imagery, typography, rules, color fields, and so on are placed with mindful intention to create focal points and to carry the viewer's eye through the piece. An underlying grid helps bring order to a progression of pages. Keeping an element of surprise and variation is key to sustaining interest.

walking down

the block

looking for

something

seeing

all

the

city lights

bells

fin
bo
ok

fin
bo
ok

Found Rhythms In this project, designers cut a 2.5-inch square cleanly through a magazine, yielding dozens of unexpected compositions. Each designer used ten of these small squares as imagery in an accordion book. The squares were scanned at 200% and placed into a page layout file (formatted in 5-inch-square pages) and paired with a text gathered from Wikipedia.

Each designer created a visual "story" by considering the pacing and scale of the images and text within each spread and across the entire sequence. Working with found or accidental content frees designers to think abstractly. Molly Hausmann, Typography I. Jeremy Botts, faculty.

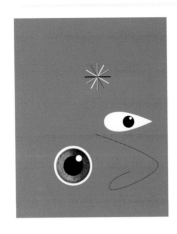
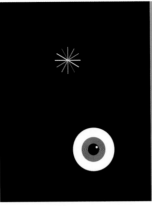

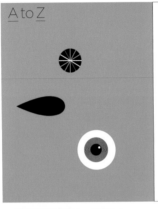

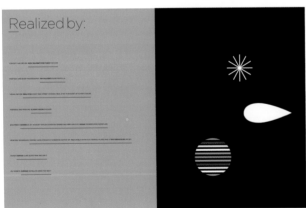

Graceful Entry These pages serve as the cover, lead in, and close of a lavishly designed and illustrated alphabet book. The simple, well-balanced elements are introduced, then animated with color and context, and finally returned to abstraction, creating a playful and compelling progression that belies the complexity of the book's interior. Rick Valicenti, Thirst.

Beautiful

The pictures
were taken fron
in either Ma**Northrup**
Chicago, I
Charlottesvi

Michael in this book
m 1976 to 1982
rietta, Ohio;
[llinois; or
lle, Virginia.

l Ecstasy

Spinal Orientation This collection of
photographs by Michael Northrup includes
many images with a prominent central
feature. Designer Paul Sahre responded
to this condition by splitting the title and
other opening text matter between the
front and back of the book, thus creating
surprise for and increased interaction with
the reader. Paul Sahre, Office of Paul Sahre.
Book photographed by Dan Meyers.

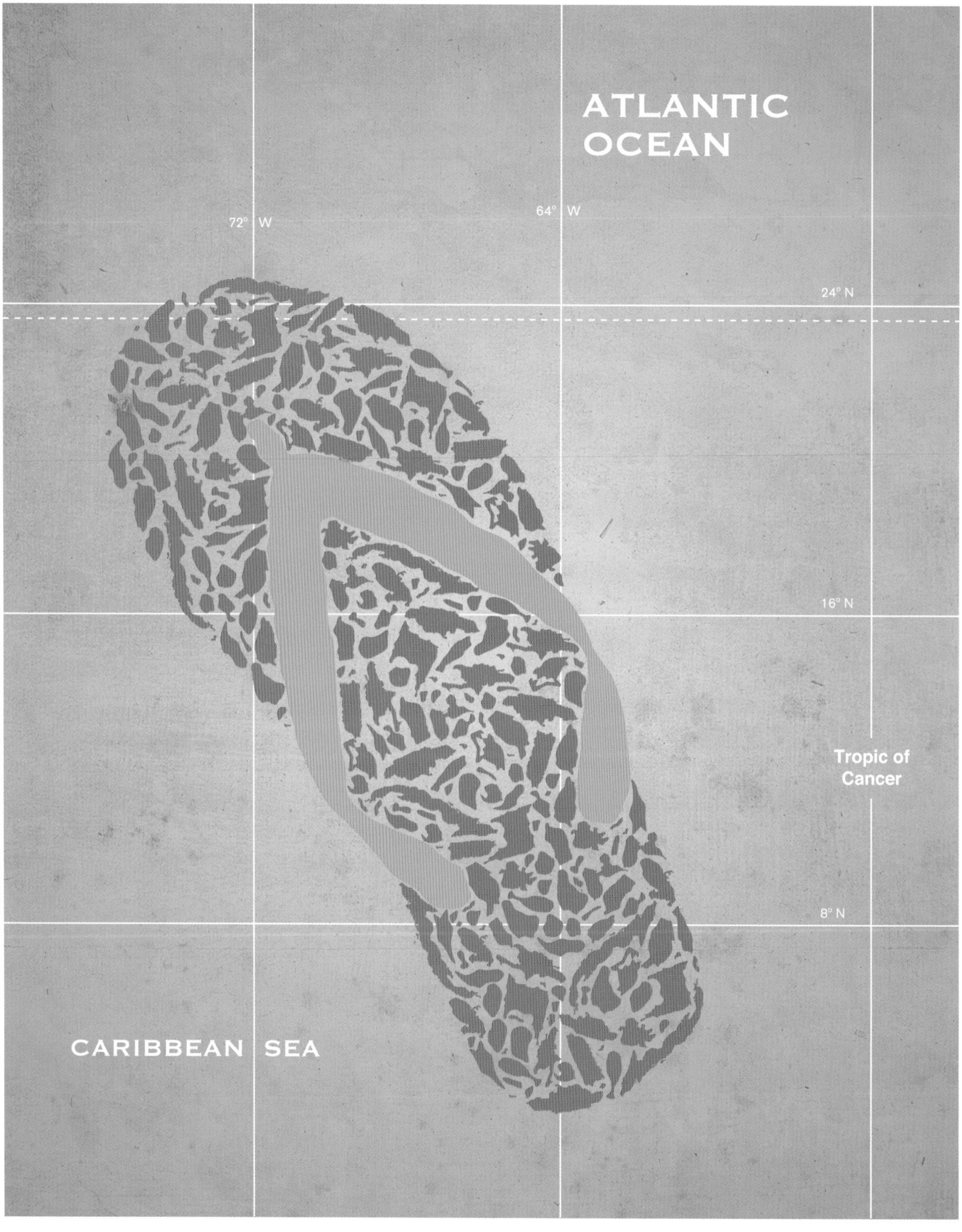

ATLANTIC
OCEAN

72° W   64° W

24° N

16° N

Tropic of
Cancer

8° N

CARIBBEAN SEA

Scale

Miss Darcy was tall, and on **a larger scale** than Elizabeth; and, though little more than sixteen, her figure was formed, and her appearance womanly and graceful. Jane Austen

A printed piece can be as small as a postage stamp or as large as a billboard. A logo must be legible both at a tiny size and from a great distance, while a film might be viewed in a huge stadium or on a handheld device. Some projects are designed to be reproduced at multiple scales, while others are conceived for a single site or medium. No matter what size your work will ultimately be, it must have its own sense of scale.

What do designers mean by scale? Scale can be considered both objectively and subjectively. In objective terms, scale refers to the literal dimensions of a physical object or to the literal correlation between a representation and the real thing it depicts. Printed maps have an exact scale: an increment of measure on the page represents an increment in the physical world. Scale models re-create relationships found in full-scale objects. Thus a model car closely approximates the features of a working vehicle, while a toy car plays with size relationships, inflating some elements while diminishing others.

Subjectively, scale refers to one's impression of an object's size. A book or a room, for example, might have a grand or intimate scale, reflecting how it relates to our own bodies and to our knowledge of other books and other rooms. We say that an image or representation "lacks scale" when it has no cues that connect it to lived experience, giving it a physical identity. A design whose elements all have a similar size often feels dull and static, lacking contrast in scale.

Scale can depend on context. An ordinary piece of paper can contain lettering or images that seem to burst off its edges, conveying a surprising sense of scale. Likewise, a small isolated element can punctuate a large surface, drawing importance from the vast space surrounding it.

Designers are often unpleasantly surprised when they first print out a piece that they have been designing on screen; elements that looked vibrant and dynamic on screen may appear dull and flaccid on the page. For example, 12pt type generally appears legible and appropriately scaled when viewed on a computer monitor, but the same type can feel crude and unwieldy as printed text. Developing sensitivity to scale is an ongoing process for every designer.

Big Picture from Small Parts This design represents Caribbean culture as the colloquy of numerous small islands. The meaning of the image comes directly from the contrast in scale. Robert Lewis, MFA Studio.

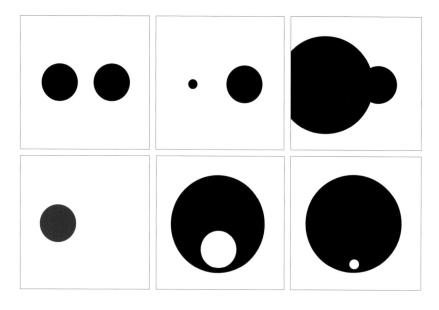

Scale is Relative

A graphic element can appear larger or smaller depending on the size, placement, and color of the elements around it. When elements are all the same size, the design feels flat. Contrast in size can create a sense of tension as well as a feeling of depth and movement. Small shapes tend to recede; large ones move forward.

Cropping to Imply Scale The larger circular form seems especially big because it bleeds off the edges of the page.

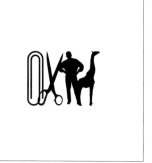

Familiar Objects, Familiar Scale We expect some objects to be a particular scale in relation to each other. Playing with that scale can create spatial illusions and conceptual relationships. Gregory May, MFA Studio.

Krista Quick, Nan Yi, Julie Diewald

Jie Lian, Sueyun Choi, Ryan Artell

Jenn Julian, Nan Yi, Sueyun Choi

Scale, Depth, and Motion In the typographic compositions shown here, designers worked with one word or a pair of words and used changes in scale as well as placement on the page to convey the meaning of the word or word pair. Contrasts in scale can imply motion or depth as well as express differences in importance.

Typography I and Graphic Design I. Ellen Lupton and Zvezdana Rogic, faculty.

Big Type, Small Pages In this book designed by Mieke Gerritzen, the small trim size of the page contrasts with the large-scale type. The surprising size of the text gives the book its loud and zealous voice. The cover is reproduced here at actual size (1:1 scale). Mieke Gerritzen and Geert Lovink, *Mobile Minded*, 2002.

e mobil
le mobi
ile mob
bile mo
obi lem

WHEN WAS THE LAST TIME
I HEARD FROM YOU ANYWAY?

058

MILBI TOY

SEND SMS

3337772633_
99966688777_
6444663

007

ONLY in JAPAN

WHERE MEN TEND TO VIEW CELLPHONES AS **TOYS,** WOMAN TREAT THEM LIKE **ACCESSORIES**

IMODE: NTT DOCOMO END-USER PRODUCT + HTML INFRASTRUCTURE

PERSONALSPACE
JUNKSPACE
VIRTUALSPACE
CELLSPACE
VISUALSPACE
FREESPACE
PUBLICSPACE
NETWO___PACE
SOC___ACE
COMM___PACE
WOR___ACE
CYBERSPACE
SMARTSPACE
AUGMENTEDSPACE

American reluctance to use mobile phones largely hinges on a highly developed sense of privacy and individuality. Just as people from more social, interconnected cultures see mobiles as a way of extending their networks and adding to their collectivity, many Americans seem to fear that the mobile will undermine their self-reliance and their independence, as well as disturbing their personal space.

THE 1990'S WERE ABOUT THE VIRTUAL:

VIRTUAL REALITY
VIRTUAL WORLDS
CYBERSPACE
AND DOT COMS

The image of an escape into a virtual world which would leave the physical space useless dominated the decade. The new decade brings with it a new emphasis on a physical space augmented with electronic, network and computer technologies: GPG; the omnipresence of video surveillance; "cellspace" applications; objects and buildings sending information to your cellphone or PDA when you are in their vicinity; and gradual dissemination of larger and flatter computer/video displays in public spaces.

SAY GOODBYE,
VIRTUAL SPACE.
PREPARE TO LIVE IN
AUGMENTED SPACE.

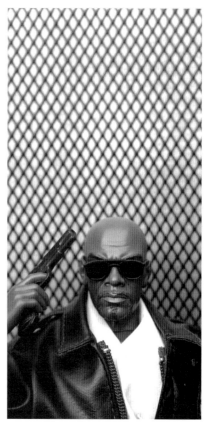

Ambiguous Scale These portraits of toy action figures play with the viewer's expectations about scale. Spatial cues reveal the actual scale of the figures; cropping out recognizable objects keeps the illusion alive. Yong Seuk Lee, MFA Studio. Abbott Miller, faculty.

Point of View Photographing small objects
up close and from a low vantage point
creates an illusion of monumentality.
Kim Bentley, MFA Studio. Abbott Miller,
faculty.

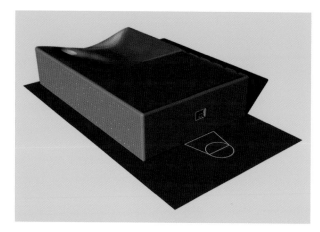

Absence of Scale This electrical utility building designed by NL Architects in Utrecht, Netherlands, has no windows or doors to indicate its scale relative to human beings or to familiar building types. The basketball hoop is the only clue to the size of this enigmatic structure. NL Architects, Netherlands, in cooperation with Bureau Nieuwbouw Centrales UNA N.V., 1997–98.

Inflated Scale In this design for an exhibition about the history of elevators and escalators, a graphic icon is blown up to an enormous scale, becoming the backdrop for a screening area in the gallery. Abbott Miller and Jeremy Hoffman, Pentagram.

Environmental Typography For an exhibition celebrating the history of *Rolling Stone*, the designers made showcases out of large-scale letterforms taken from the magazine's distinctive logotype. Abbott Miller and James Hicks, Pentagram.

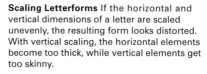

Scale is a Verb

To scale a graphic element is to change its dimensions. Software makes it easy to scale photographs, vector graphics, and letterforms. Changing the scale of an element can transform its impact on the page or screen. Be careful, however: it's easy to distort an element by scaling it disproportionately.

Vector graphics are scalable, meaning that they can be enlarged or reduced without degrading the quality of the image. Bitmap images cannot be enlarged without resulting in a soft or jaggy image.

In two-dimensional animation, enlarging a graphic object over time can create the appearance of a zoom, as if the object were moving closer to the screen.

Scaling Letterforms If the horizontal and vertical dimensions of a letter are scaled unevenly, the resulting form looks distorted. With vertical scaling, the horizontal elements become too thick, while vertical elements get too skinny.

With horizontal scaling, vertical elements become disproportionately heavy, while horizontal elements get thin.

AAAAAAAAAA

Full-Range Type Family Many typefaces include variations designed with different proportions. The Helvetica Neue type family includes light, medium, bold, and black letters in normal, condensed, and extended widths. The strokes of each letter appear uniform. That effect is destroyed if the letters are unevenly scaled.

| Correct Proportions | Horizontal Scaling | Vertical Scaling |

Scaling Images and Objects Uneven scaling distorts images as well as typefaces. Imagine if you could scale a physical object, stretching or squashing it to make it fit into a particular space. The results are not pretty. Eric Karnes.

Extreme Heights In the poster at right for a lecture at a college, designer Paul Sahre put his typography under severe pressure, yielding virtually illegible results. (He knew he had a captive audience.) Paul Sahre.

PAUL SAHRE: EXERCISES IN FUTILITY, PART IV

APRIL 7, 2000 4PM BUNTING 110 M.I.C.A.

FREE

Texture

If you touch something (it is likely) someone will feel it.
If you feel something (it is likely) **someone will be touched.**

Rick Valicenti

Texture is the tactile grain of surfaces and substances. Textures in our environment help us understand the nature of things: rose bushes have sharp thorns to protect the delicate flowers they surround; smooth, paved roads signal safe passage; thick fog casts a veil on our view.

The textures of design elements similarly correspond to their visual function. An elegant, smoothly patterned surface might adorn the built interior or printed brochure of a day spa; a snaggle of barbed wire could stand as a metaphor for violence or incarceration.

In design, texture is both physical and virtual. Textures include the literal surface employed in the making of a printed piece or physical object as well as the optical appearance of that surface. Paper can be rough or smooth, fabric can be nubby or fine, and packaging material can be glossy or matte. Physical textures affect how a piece feels to the hand, but they also affect how it looks. A smooth or glossy surface, for example, reflects light differently than a soft or pebbly one.

Many of the textures that designers manipulate are not physically experienced by the viewer at all, but exist as optical effect and representation. Texture adds detail to an image, providing an overall surface quality as well as rewarding the eye when viewed up close.

Whether setting type or depicting a tree, the designer uses texture to establish a mood, reinforce a point of view, or convey a sense of physical presence. A body of text set in Garamond italic will have a delicately irregular appearance, while a text set in Univers roman will appear optically smooth with even tonality. Likewise, a smoothly drawn vector illustration will have a different feel from an image taken with a camera or created with code.

As in life, the beauty of texture in design often lies in its poignant juxtaposition or contrast: prickly/soft, sticky/dry, fuzzy/smooth, and so on. By placing one texture in relation to its opposite, or a smart counterpart, the designer can amplify the unique formal properties of each one.

This chapter presents a wide spectrum of textures generated by hand, camera, computer, and code. They are abstract and concrete, and they have been captured, configured, sliced, built, and brushed. They were chosen to remind us that texture has a genuine, visceral, wholly seductive capacity to reel us in and hold us.

High-Tech Finger Paint The letterforms in Rick Valicenti's Touchy Feely alphabet were painted on vertical glass and recorded photographically with a long exposure from a digital, large-format Hasselblad camera. Rick Valicenti, Thirst.

Concrete Texture
The physical quality resulting from repeated slicing, burning, marking, and extracting creates concrete textural surfaces with robust appeal. The studies to the right grew out of a studio exercise where the computer was prohibited in the initial stages of concept and formal development. Turbulence (below), an alphabet by Rick Valicenti, similarly evokes a raw physicality. The alphabet began with vigorous hand-drawn, looping scribbles that were then translated into code.

Surface Manipulation The textural physicality of these type studies artfully reflects the active processes featured in the words. The crisscrossing lines of an artist's cutting board resemble an urban street grid. Jonnie Hallman, Graphic Design I. Bernard Canniffe, faculty.

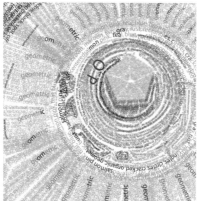

Physical and Virtual Texture
This exercise builds connections between physical and virtual texture (the feel and look of surfaces). Designers used digital cameras to capture compelling textures from the environment. Next, they wrote descriptive paragraphs about each of the textures, focusing on their images' formal characteristics.

Using these descriptive texts as content, the designers re-created the textures typographically in Adobe Illustrator, employing repetition, scale, layers, and color. Typeface selection was open, but scale distortion was not permitted.
Graphic Design I. Mike Weikert, faculty.

Hayley Griffin

Grey Haas

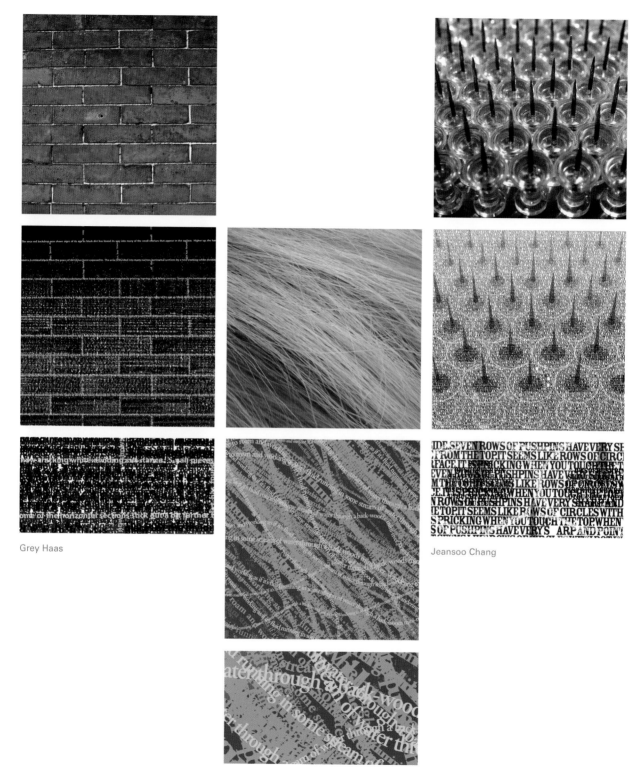

Grey Haas

Jeansoo Chang

Tim Mason

Topographic Landscape Aerial photograph
of harvested wheat fields shows indexical
traces of the process through many incised,
looping and overlapping lines. Cameron
Davidson.

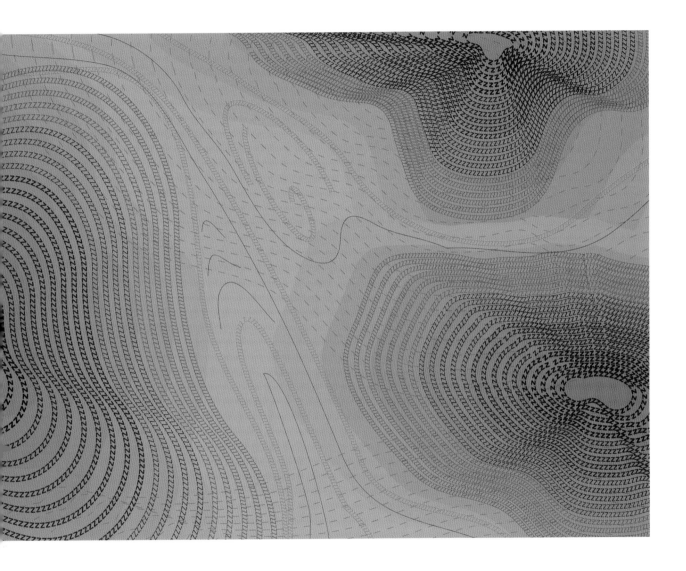

Typographic Landscape Curving lines of
text serve to build up a typographic surface,
creating the illusion of a topographic
landscape. Visakh Menon, MFA Studio.

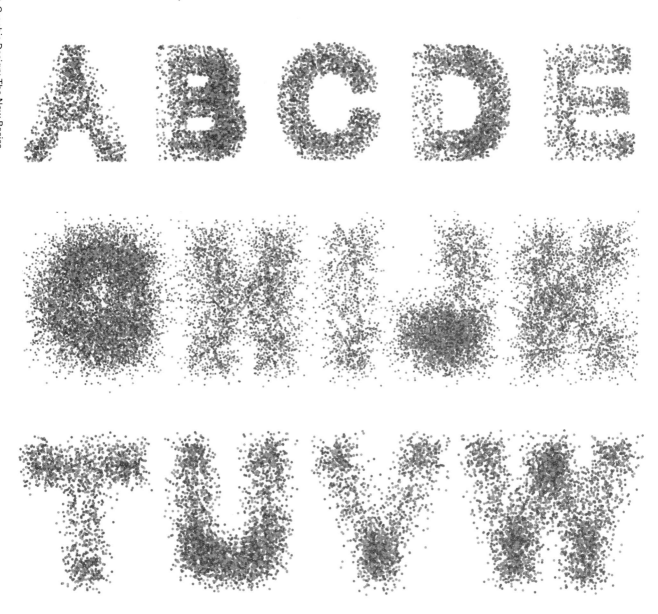

Code-Driven Texture The Swiss typographer
Emil Ruder once claimed that vital and
individual typographic rhythms are alien
to machines. The code-driven letterforms
shown here prove otherwise. Generated
in the computer language Processing, these
forms are effervescent, organic, and, indeed,
vital. Yeohyun Ahn, MFA Studio.

All About the Money The textured letters in this editorial illustration are rendered in 3D imaging software. The rhinestone-studded text is set against a Tiffany-blue sky, providing what designer Rick Valicenti calls "a suburban white male's version of the pixel pusher/gangsta aesthetic." Designer: Rick Valicenti, Thirst. Programmer: Matt Daly, Luxworks.

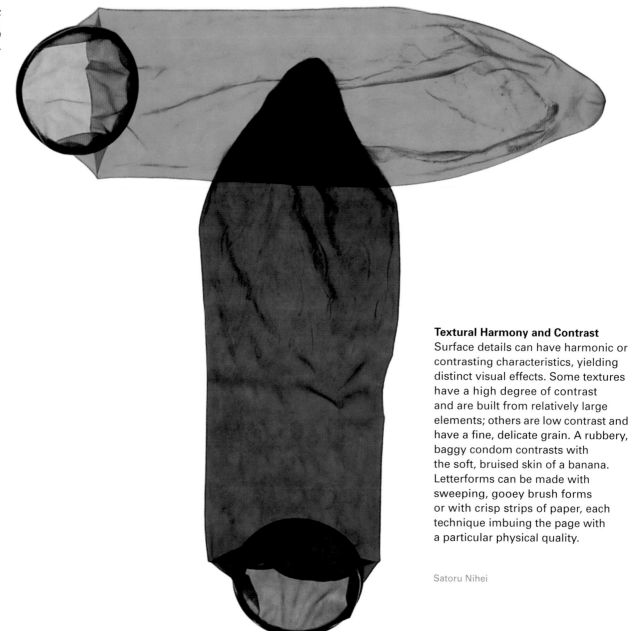

Textural Harmony and Contrast
Surface details can have harmonic or contrasting characteristics, yielding distinct visual effects. Some textures have a high degree of contrast and are built from relatively large elements; others are low contrast and have a fine, delicate grain. A rubbery, baggy condom contrasts with the soft, bruised skin of a banana. Letterforms can be made with sweeping, gooey brush forms or with crisp strips of paper, each technique imbuing the page with a particular physical quality.

Satoru Nihei

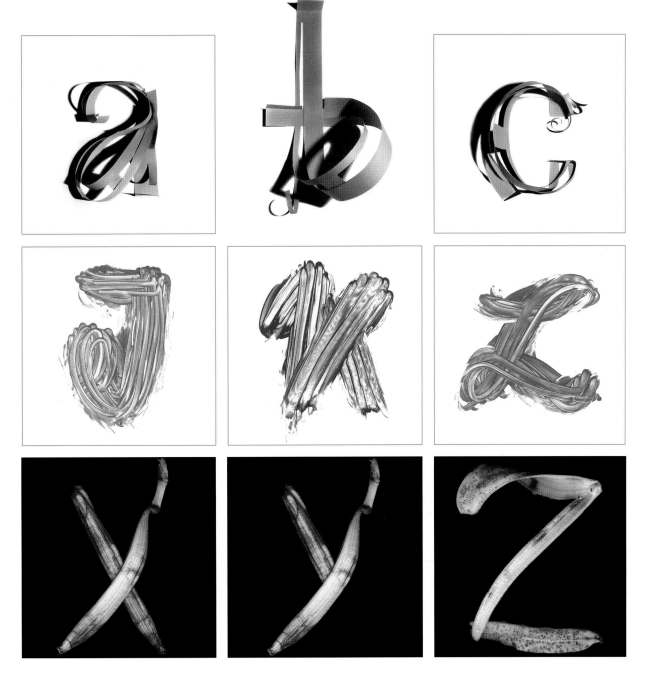

Alphabetic Texture These alphabets are from a diverse collection created for Rick Valicenti's Playground experiment, where letters are constructed from physical objects and processes. Designers top to bottom: Michelle Bowers, Rick Valicenti, Jenn Stucker.

Abbott Miller and Kristen Spilman, Pentagram

Textured Logotypes The logotypes shown here, designed by Pentagram, use textured surfaces to convey ideas of movement and change. In a logo for an exhibition about the idea of "swarming" in contemporary art, thousands of tiny elements flock together to create a larger structure. In Pentagram's visual identity for MICA, patterning provides a rich patina that resonates with the school's urban neighborhood. The main typographic mark gracefully balances tradition and innovation. Solid historical letterforms are punctuated by a modern linear framework, referencing the two architecturally significant buildings that anchor the campus—one building is classical and cubic, while the other is dramatically angled. The texture makes the logo light and engaging when it is used at a large scale.

Abbott Miller and Kristen Spilman, Pentagram

Textural Applications The MICA mark and pattern breathe life into a cardboard portfolio. The same pattern appears on works of street couture. Abbott Miller and Kristen Spilman, Pentagram. Photography: Nancy Froehlich.

Five Squares Ten Inches All typefaces have an innate optical texture that results from the accumulation of attributes such as serifs, slope, stroke width, and proportion. Those attributes interact on the page with the size, tracking, leading, and paragraph style selected by the designer, yielding an overall texture.

In this exercise, designers composed five justified squares of type inside a ten-inch frame. Variation of type style, texture, and value were achieved by combining contrasting characteristics such as old style italic serifs, uniformly weighted sans serifs, geometric slab serifs, and so on. Light to dark value (typographic color) was controlled through the combination of stroke width, letterspacing, and paragraph leading.

Finally, students manipulated the scale and placement of the squares to achieve compositional balance, tension, and depth. Squares were permitted to bleed off the edges, reinforcing the illusion of amplification and recession. Typography I. Jennifer Cole Phillips, faculty.

Julie Diewald

Anna Eshelman

ny, that hath to instrument
e never surfeited sea hath
land where man doth not
our men hang and drown
y fellous are ministers of
ords are temper'd, may as
bemock'd-at stabs kill the
dowle that's in my plume
erable. If you could hurt
our strengths and will not
y business to you, that you
Prospero, exposed unto the
s innocent child: for which
rgetting, have incensed the
against your peace. Thee
and do pronounce by me
death can be at once, shall
ys whose wraths to guard
esolate isle, else falls upon
w and a clear life ensuing

never may believe these antique
ables, nor these fairy toys. Lovers
and madmen have such seething
brains, such shaping fantasies, that
comprehend more than cool reason ever
comprehends. The lunatic, the lover
and the poet are of imagination all
compact. One sees more devils
than vast hell can hold, that is, the
madman. The lover, all as frantic, sees
Helen's beauty in a brow of Egypt: the
poet's eye, in fine frenzy rolling, doth
glance from heaven to earth, from
earth to heaven; and as imagination
bodies forth the forms of things
unknown, the poet's pen turns them
to shapes and gives to airy nothing
a local habitation and a name. Such
tricks hath strong imagination, that if
it would but apprehend some joy, it
comprehends some bringer of that joy

Anna Eshelman

y mouth tastes like menthol, newly minted coins, and
blood. the flavor of clean. flossed and metallic, french
kissing a robot. You told me something wednesday night
that made me chirp and glow. Do you know you do
that? Your love is one to revel in. You mean so many subtle
things. Like the way wassail burns the back of your throat
et draws you back for more. Like waking up and keeping
your eyes closed and your heartrate low. Like the color of
he sky when it snows. Like that second when the blades
n a ceiling fan finally come to a smooth halt. you embody
everything i have ever known, loved, and stored
n mind If I were a transformer, I'd fold into a cat. Maybe.

**My mouth tastes like menthol, newly minted
coins, and blood. the flavor of clean. flossed
and metallic, french kissing a robot. You told
me something wednesday night that made me
chirp and glow. Do you know you do that?
Your love is one to revel in. You mean so
many subtle things. Like the way wassail
burns the back of your throat, but draws you
back for more. like waking up and keeping
your eyes closed and your heartrate low. like
the color of the sky when it snows. like that
second when the blades on a ceiling fan finally
burns the back of your throat, but draws you
back for more. like waking up and keeping
your eyes closed and your heartrate low. like
burns the back of your throat, but draws you
closed and your heartrate low. like come**

My mouth tastes like menthol, newly minted
coins, and blood. the flavor of clean. flossed
and metallic, french kissing a robot. You told
me something wednesday night that made me
chirp and glow. Do you know you do that?
Your love is one to revel in. You mean so many
subtle things. Like the way wassail burns the
back of your throat, but draws you back for
more. like waking up and keeping your eyes
closed and your heartrate low. like the color
of the sky when it snows. like that second when
the blades on a ceiling fan finally come to a
smooth halt. you embody everything i have
ever known, loved, and stored in mind. If I
were a transformer, I'd fold into a cat. Maybe

MY MOUTH TASTES LIKE MENTHOL, NEWL
MINTED COINS, AND BLOOD. THE FLAVO
OF CLEAN. FLOSSED AND METALLIC, FRENDI
KISSING A ROBOT. YOU TOLD ME SOMETHIN
WEDNESDAY NIGHT THAT MADE ME CHIRI
AND GLOW. DO YOU KNOW YOU DO THAT
YOUR LOVE IS ONE TO REVEL IN. YOU MEAN
SO MANY SUBTLE THINGS. LIKE THE WAY
WASSAIL BURNS THE BACK OF YOUR THROAT
BUT DRAWS YOU BACK FOR MORE. LIKE WAKIN
UP AND KEEPING YOUR EYES CLOSED AND YOUR
YOUR HEARTRATE LOW. LIKE THE COLOR O
THE SKY WHEN IT SNOWS. LIKE THAT SECON
WHEN THE BLADES ON A CEILING FAN
FINALLY COME TO A SMOOTH HALT. YO
EMBODY EVERYTHING I HAVE EVER KNOWN
LOVED, AND STORED IN MIND. IF I WERE
TRANSFORMER, I'D FOLD INTO A CAT. MAYBE

Ellen Kling

**At the Pentagon, Defense Secretary Donald H
Rumsfeld said that while it was unclear what
role the U.S. military might take in enforcing
new U.N. sanctions, he did not expect the United
States or any other nation to do so unilaterally
At the Pentagon, Defense Secretary Donald H
Rumsfeld said that while it was unclear what
role the U.S. military might take in enforcing
new U.N. sanctions, he did not expect the United
States or any other nation to do so unilaterally
At the Pentagon, Defense Secretary Donald H
Rumsfeld said that while it was unclear what
role the U.S. military might take in enforcing
new U.N. sanctions, he did not expect the United
States or any other nation to do so unilaterally
At the Pentagon, Defense Secretary Donald H
Rumsfeld said that while it was unclear what
role the U.S. military might take in enforcing
new U.N. sanctions, he did not expect the United**

*At the Pentagon, Defense Secretary Donald H Rumsfeld
said that while it was unclear what role the U.S. military
might take in enforcing new U.N. sanctions, he did
not expect the United States or any other nation to do so
At the Pentagon, Defense Secretary Donald H Rumsfeld
said that while it was unclear what role the U.S. military
might take in enforcing new U.N. sanctions, he did
not expect the United States or any other nation to do so
At the Pentagon, Defense Secretary Donald H Rumsfeld
said that while it was unclear what role the U.S. military
might take in enforcing new U.N. sanctions, he did
not expect the United States or any other nation to do so
At the Pentagon, Defense Secretary Donald H Rumsfeld
said that while it was unclear what role the U.S. military
might take in enforcing new U.N. sanctions, he did*

HyunSoo Lim

**On Wednesday, owners and workers downtown
boom shattering glass Everyone first feared add
another These fears were quickly dispelled mad
when sources noise traveled into sight fighters ad
Witnesses couldn't believe their eyes Building its
sized vegetables were bouncing down the foxes
street smashing things that got into their wand
Small found throughout city had begun vegetable
their Southern some unseen force dervish fusion
levitated tarnish and into the streets water cared
humongous siblings Fire trucks and cops sandy
shoot down hose down, and rope down every an
traffic hazards Nothing worked. vegetables alter
only leaked lifesize seeds tons of juice onto most
buildings, pedestrians streets. The parade of lost
vegetables apparently was first spotted upper
Manhattan and traveled all the way to the Statue
Liberty, where they then moved out to sea. Most
three hours the parade had managed structurally
damage thirty five buildings, scare the population
of the New York City, and leave them without add
vegetables for potentially a week (a scary thought**

ass, and tell the face thou viewest Now
face should form another Whose fresh
thou not renewest Thou dost beguile
pless some mother For where is she so
ear'd womb Disdains the tillage of
Or who is he so fond will be the tomb
, to stop posterity Thou art thy mother's
e in thee Calls back the lovely April
so thou through windows of thine age
ite of wrinkles this thy golden time But
member'd not to be Die single, and
ies with thee Look in thy glass, tell the

day Thou art more lovely and m
temperate Rough winds do sha
the darling buds of May And m
summer's lease hath all too shor
a date Sometime too hot the e
of heaven shines And often is
gold complexion dimm'd And ev
fair from fair sometime declines
chance or nature's changing cou
untrimm'd But thy eternal summ
shall not fade Nor lose possess
of that fair thou owest Nor shal
Death brag thou wander'st in th
shade When in eternal lines to t
thou growest So long as men ca
breathe or eyes can see So long
lives this and this gives life to th

Julie Diewald

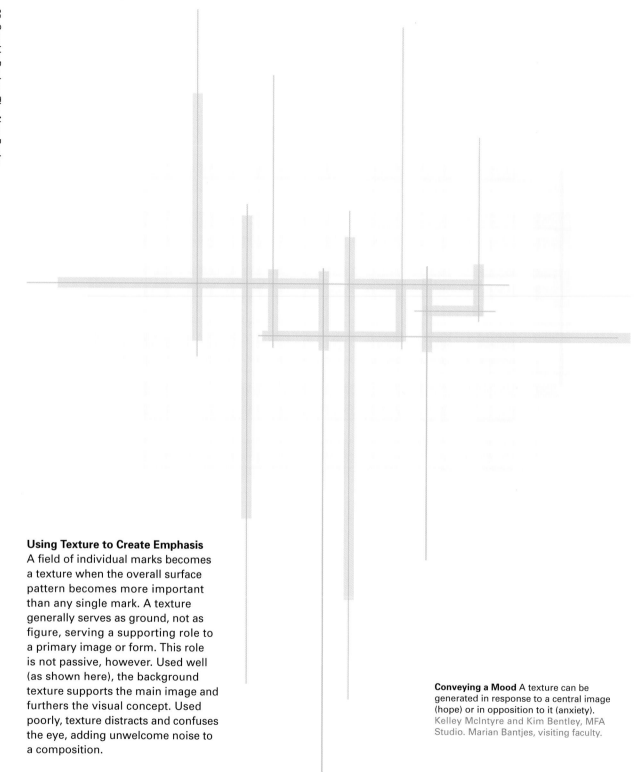

Using Texture to Create Emphasis
A field of individual marks becomes
a texture when the overall surface
pattern becomes more important
than any single mark. A texture
generally serves as ground, not as
figure, serving a supporting role to
a primary image or form. This role
is not passive, however. Used well
(as shown here), the background
texture supports the main image and
furthers the visual concept. Used
poorly, texture distracts and confuses
the eye, adding unwelcome noise to
a composition.

Conveying a Mood A texture can be
generated in response to a central image
(hope) or in opposition to it (anxiety).
Kelley McIntyre and Kim Bentley, MFA
Studio. Marian Bantjes, visiting faculty.

Color

All colors are the friends of their neighbors
and the **lovers of their opposites**. Marc Chagall

Color can convey a mood, describe reality, or codify information. Words like "gloomy," "drab," and "glittering" each bring to mind a general climate of colors, a palette of relationships. Designers use color to make some things stand out (warning signs) and to make other things disappear (camouflage). Color serves to differentiate and connect, to highlight and to hide.

Graphic design was once seen as a fundamentally black-and-white enterprise. This is no longer the case. Color has become integral to the design process. Color printing, once a luxury, has become routine. An infinite range of hues and intensities bring modern media to life, energizing the page, the screen, and the built environment with sensuality and significance. Graphics and color have converged.

According to the classical tradition, the essence of design lies in linear structures and tonal relationships (drawing and shading), not in fleeting optical effects (hue, intensity, luminosity). Design used to be understood as an abstract armature that underlies appearances. Color, in contrast, was seen as subjective and unstable.

And, indeed, it is. Color exists, literally, in the eye of the beholder. We cannot perceive color until light bounces off an object or is emitted from a source and enters the eye.

Our perception of color depends not solely on the pigmentation of physical surfaces, but also on the brightness and character of ambient light. We also perceive a given color in relation to the other colors around it. For example, a light tone looks lighter against a dark ground than against a pale one.

Likewise, color changes meaning from culture to culture. Colors carry different connotations in different societies. White signals virginity and purity in the West, but it is the color of death in Eastern cultures. Red, worn by brides in Japan, is considered racy and erotic in Europe and the United States. Colors go in and out of fashion, and an entire industry has emerged to guide and predict its course.

To say, however, that color is a shifting phenomenon—both physically and culturally—is not to say that it can't be described or understood. A precise vocabulary has been established over time that makes it possible for designers, software systems, printers, and manufacturers to communicate to one another with some degree of clarity. This chapter outlines the basic terms of color theory and shows ways to build purposeful relationships among colors.

Opposites Attract Strong color contrasts add visual energy to this dense physical montage made from flowers. Blue and purple stand out against pink, orange, and red. Nancy Froehlich and Zvezdana Rogic.

Basic Color Theory
In 1665 Sir Isaac Newton discovered that a prism separates light into the spectrum of colors: red, orange, yellow, green, blue, indigo, and violet. He organized the colors around a wheel very much like the one artists use today to describe the relationships among colors.[1]

Why is the color wheel a useful design tool? Colors that sit near each other on the spectrum or close together on the color wheel are analogous. Using them together provides minimal color contrast and an innate harmony, because each color has some element in common with others in the sequence. Analogous colors also have a related color temperature. Two colors sitting opposite each other on the wheel are complements. Each color contains no element of the other, and they have opposing temperatures (warm versus cool). Deciding to use analogous or contrasting colors affects the visual energy and mood of any composition.

Complementary and Analogous Colors
This diagram shows combinations of primary, secondary, and tertiary colors.
Robert Lewis, MFA Studio.

1. On basic color theory and practice, see Tom Fraser and Adam Banks, *Designer's Color Manual* (San Francisco: Chronicle Books, 2004).

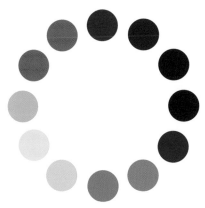

The Color Wheel
This basic map shows relationships among colors. Children learn to mix colors according to this model, and artists use it for working with pigments (oil paint, watercolor, gouache, and so on).

Primary Colors
Red, yellow, and blue are pure; they can't be mixed from other colors. All of the other colors on the wheel are created by mixing primary colors.

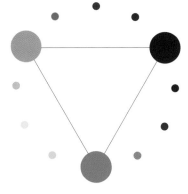

Secondary Colors
Orange, purple, and green each consist of two primaries mixed together.

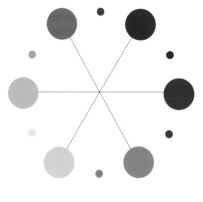

Tertiary Colors
Colors such as red orange and yellow green are mixed from one primary and one secondary color.

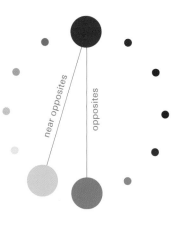

near opposites

opposites

Complements
Red/green, blue/orange, and yellow/purple sit opposite each other on the color wheel. For more subtle combinations, choose "near opposites," such as red plus a tertiary green, or a tertiary blue and a tertiary orange.

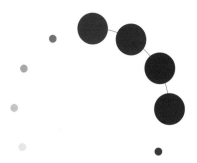

Analogous Colors
Color schemes built from hues that sit near to each other on the color wheel (analogous colors) have minimal chromatic differences.

Hue is the place of the color within the spectrum. A red hue can look brown at a low saturation, or pink at a pale value.

Intensity is the brightness or dullness of a color. A color is made duller by adding black or white, as well as by neutralizing it toward gray (lowering its saturation).

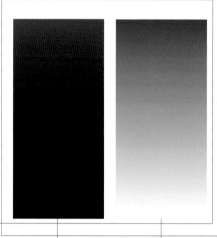

Value is the light or dark character of the color, also called its luminance, brightness, lightness, or tone. Value is independent of the hue or intensity of the color. When you convert a color image to black and white, you eliminate its hue but preserve its tonal relationships.

Aspects of Color

Every color can be described in relation to a range of attributes. Understanding these characteristics can help you make color choices and build color combinations. Using colors with contrasting values tends to bring forms into sharp focus, while combining colors that are close in value softens the distinction between elements.

Shade is a variation of a hue produced by the addition of black.

Tint is a variation of a hue produced by the addition of white.

Saturation (also called chroma) is the relative purity of the color as it neutralizes to gray.

These colors are close in value and intensity, and just slightly different in hue.

These colors are close in hue and value but different in intensity.

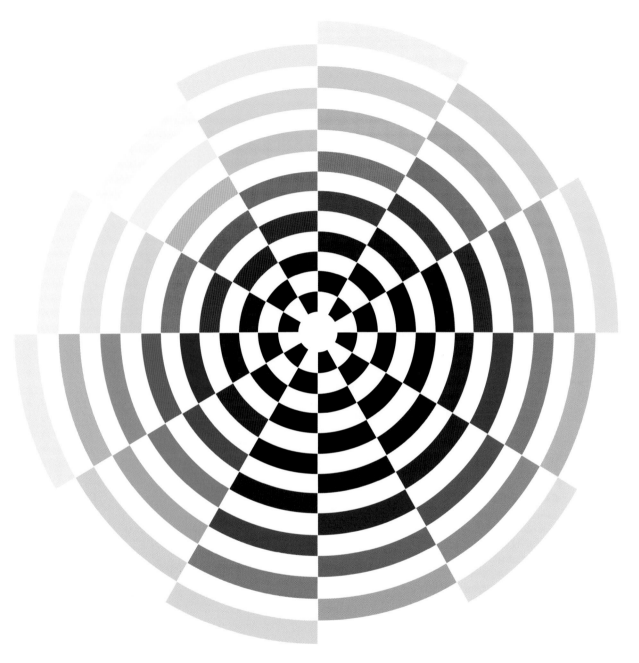

Graduated Color Wheel Each hue on the color wheel is shown here in a progressive series of values (shades and tints). Note that the point of greatest saturation is not the same for each hue. Yellow is of greatest intensity toward the lighter end of the value scale, while blue is more intense in the darker zone.

Use the graduated color wheel to look for combinations of colors that are similar in value or saturation, or use it to build contrasting relationships. Robert Lewis, MFA Studio.

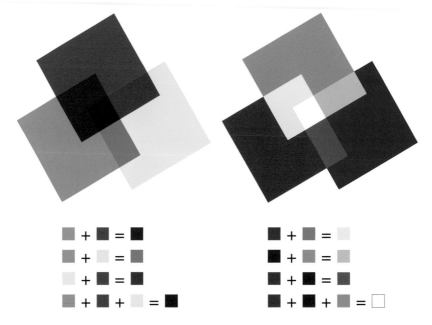

Color Models

Surfaces absorb certain light waves and reflect back others onto the color receptors (cones) in our eyes. The light reflected back is the light we see. The true primaries of visible light are red, green, and blue. The light system is called "additive" because the three primaries together create all the hues in the spectrum.

In theory, combining red and green paint should produce yellow. In practice, however, these pigments combine into a blackish brown. This is because pigments absorb more light than they reflect, making any mix of pigments darker than its source colors. As more colors are mixed, less light is reflected. Thus pigment-based color systems are called "subtractive."

Offset and desktop printing methods use CMYK, a subtractive system. Nonstandard colors are used because the light reflected off cyan and magenta pigments mixes more purely into new hues than the light reflected off of blue and red pigments.

CYMK is used in the printing process. While painters use the basic color wheel as a guide for mixing paint, printing ink uses a different set of colors: cyan, magenta, yellow, and black, which are ideal for reproducing the range of colors found in color photographs. C, M, Y, and K are known as the "process colors," and full-color printing is called "four-color process." Ink-jet and color laser printers use CMYK, as does the commercial offset printing equipment used to print books such as this one.

In principle, C, M, and Y should produce black, but the resulting mix is not rich enough to reproduce color images with a full tonal range. Thus black is needed to complete the four-color process.

RGB is the additive system used for designing on screen. Different percentages of red, green, and blue light combine to generate the colors of the spectrum. White occurs when all three colors are at full strength. Black occurs when zero light (and thus zero color) is emitted.

Any given color can be described with both CMYK and RGB values, as well as with other color models. Each model (called a "color space") uses numbers to convey color information uniformly around the globe and across media. Different monitors, printing conditions, and paper stocks all affect the appearance of the final color, as does the light in the environment where the color is viewed. Colors look different under fluorescent, incandescent, and natural light. Colors rarely translate perfectly from one space to another.

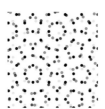

Transparent Ink Printer's inks are transparent, so color mixing occurs as colors show through each other. Color mixing is also performed optically when the image is broken down into tiny dots of varying size. The resulting colors are mixed by the eye.

Transparent Light The medium of light is also transparent. The colors of an emitted image are generated when different colors of light mix directly, as well as when tiny adjacent pixels combine optically.

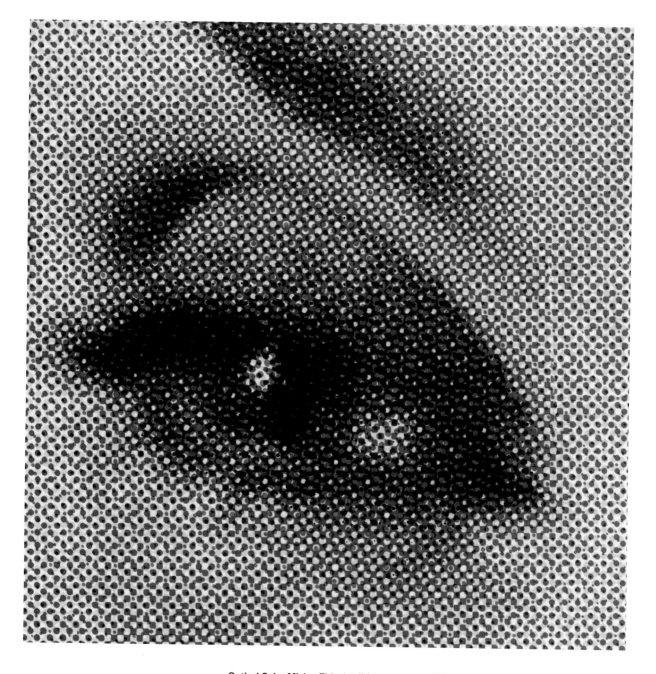

Optical Color Mixing This detail from a printed paper billboard shows the principle of four-color process printing (CMYK). Viewed from a distance, the flecks of color mix together optically. Seen up close, the pattern of dots is strongly evident.

Whatever color model your software is using, if you are viewing it on screen, it is RGB. If you are viewing it in print, it is CMYK.

One Color, Different Effects The neutral tone passing through these three squares of color is the same in each instance. It takes on a slightly different hue or value depending on its context.

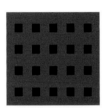

Bezold Effect Johann Friedrich Wilhelm von Bezold was a German physicist working in the nineteenth century. Fascinated with light and color, he also was an amateur rug maker. He noticed that by changing a color that interwove with other colors in a rug, he could create entirely different results. Adding a darker color to the carpet would create an overall darker effect, while adding a lighter one yielded a lighter carpet. This effect is known as optical mixing.

Interaction of Color

Josef Albers, a painter and designer who worked at the Bauhaus before emigrating the United States, studied color in a rigorous manner that influenced generations of art educators.[2] Giving his students preprinted sheets of colored paper with which to work, he led them to analyze and experience how the perception of color changes in relation to how any given color is juxtaposed with others.

Colors are mixed in the eye as well as directly on the painter's palette or the printing press. This fact affects how designers create patterns and textures, and it is exploited in digital and mechanical printing methods, which use small flecks of pure hue to build up countless color variations.

Designers juxtapose colors to create specific climates and qualities, using one color to diminish or intensify another. Understanding how colors interact helps designers control the power of color and systematically test variations of an idea.

2. See Josef Albers, *Interaction of Color* (1963; repr., New Haven: Yale University Press, 2006).

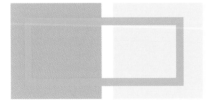

Vibration and Value When two colors are very close in value, a glowing effect occurs; on the left, the green appears luminous and unstable. With a strong value difference, as seen on the right, the green appears darker.

Color + White

Color + Black

Color + Gray

Complements

Near Complements

Analogous Colors

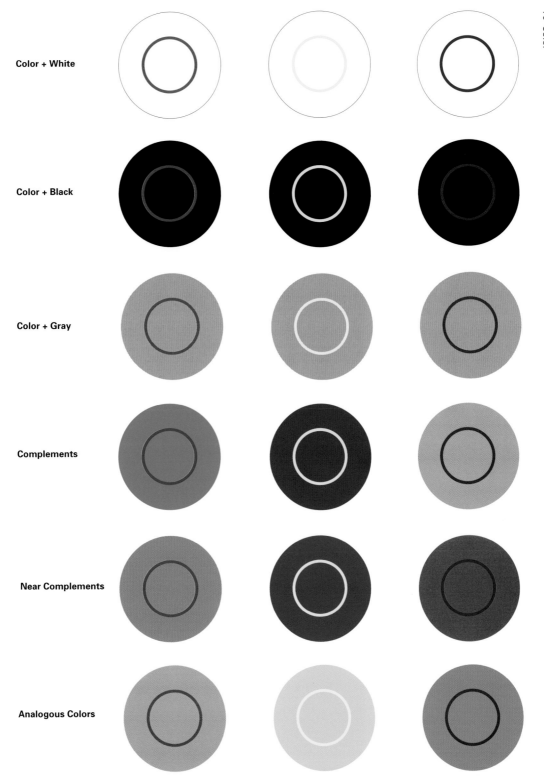

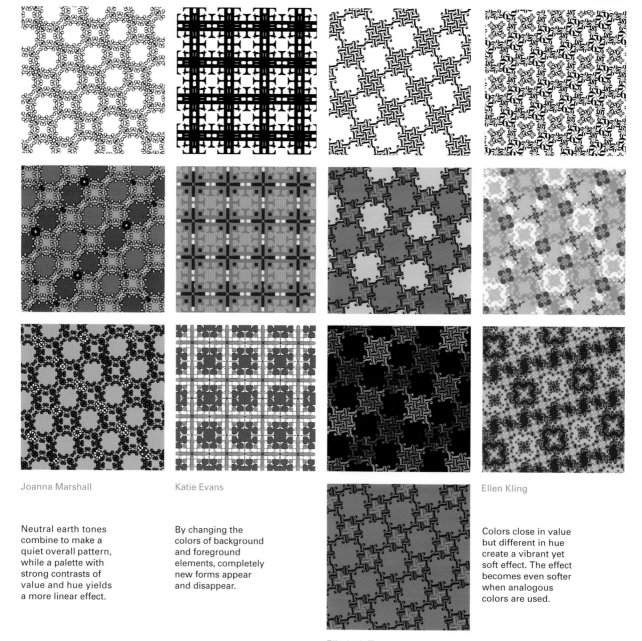

Joanna Marshall

Katie Evans

Ellen Kling

Elizabeth Tipson

Neutral earth tones combine to make a quiet overall pattern, while a palette with strong contrasts of value and hue yields a more linear effect.

By changing the colors of background and foreground elements, completely new forms appear and disappear.

Colors close in value but different in hue create a vibrant yet soft effect. The effect becomes even softer when analogous colors are used.

Selective Emphasis These studies use typographic pattern to explore how color alters not just the mood of a pattern, but the way its shapes and figures are perceived. Color affects both the parts and the whole. Each study begins with a black and white pattern built from a single font and letterform.

Experiments with hue, value, and saturation, as well as with analogous, complementary, and near complementary color juxtapositions, affect the way the patterns feel and behave. Through selective emphasis, some elements pull forward and others recede. Typography I. Jennifer Cole Phillips, faculty.

Anna Eshelman

Julie Diewald

Anna Eshelman

Anna Eshelman

The similarly muted
hues of olive
and brown sit back,
allowing a pale
yellow pattern to
come forward.
Next, gradations of
yellow, orange, and
red weave through
a green background
of equivalent value,
causing the dark blue
shapes to command
attention.

In the first color
study above, the
complementary
orange and blue
squares vibrate
against each other,
while the analogous
yellow and green
play a more passive
role. In the second
study, the dark blue
and burgundy tones
frame and push
forward the brighter
blues in the center.

The muted neutral
hues allow the forms
to gently commingle,
while contrasting
hues and values break
the elements apart.

Passion, Palettes, and Products What began as a love for Portuguese tile patterns on a trip to Lisbon evolved into an intensive investigation into pattern, form, and color, manifesting itself in an MFA thesis project and now an online business.

Textile designers often create numerous color ways for a single pattern, allowing the same printing plates or weaving templates to generate diverse patterns. Different color palettes make different elements of the pattern come forward or recede. Jessica Pilar, MFA Studio.

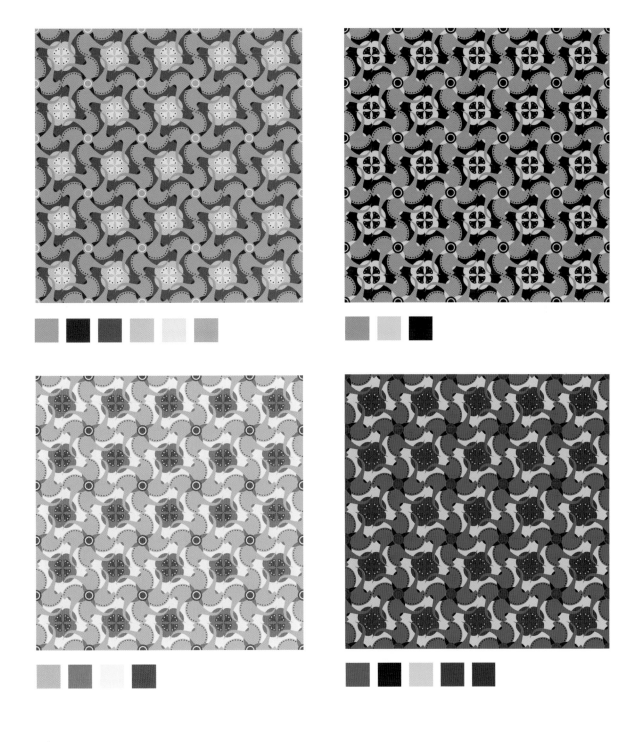

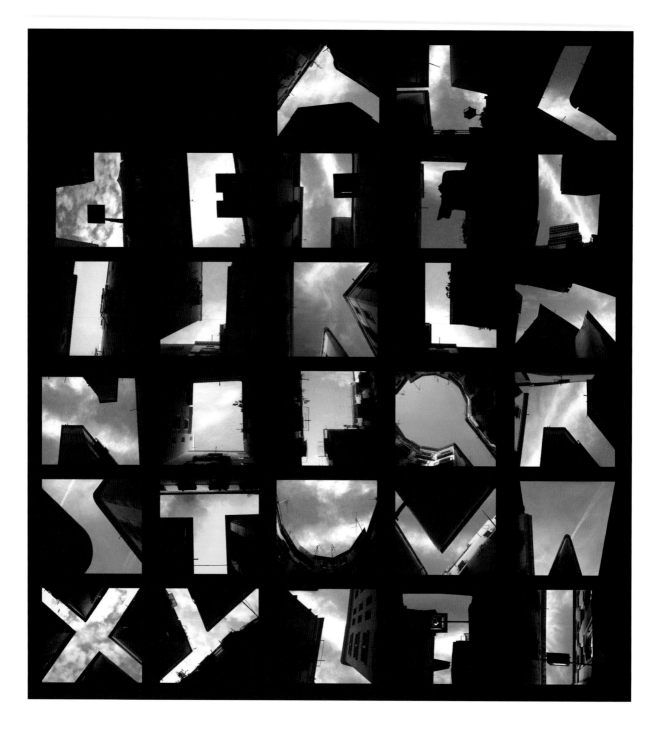

The form of an object is not more important than the form of the space surrounding it. **All things exist in interaction with other things.** In music, are the separations between notes less important than the notes themselves? Malcolm Grear

Figure/ground relationships shape visual perception. A figure (form) is always seen in relation to what surrounds it (ground, or background)—letters to a page, a building to its site, a sculpture to the space within it and around it, the subject of a photograph to its setting, and so on. A black shape on a black field is not visible; without separation and contrast, form disappears.

People are accustomed to seeing the background as passive and unimportant in relation to a dominant subject. Yet visual artists quickly become attuned to the spaces around and between elements, discovering their power to shape experience and become active forms in their own right.

Graphic designers often seek a balance between figure and ground, using this relationship to bring energy and order to form and space. They build contrasts between form and counterform in order to construct icons, illustrations, logos, compositions, and patterns that stimulate the eye. Creating figure/ground tension or ambiguity adds visual energy to an image or mark. Even subtle ambiguity can invigorate the end result and shift its direction and impact.

Figure/ground, also known as positive and negative space, is at work in all facets of graphic design. In the design of logotypes and symbols, the distillation of complex meaning into simplified but significant form often thrives on the taut reciprocity of figure and ground. In posters, layouts, and screen designs, what is left out frames and balances what is built in. Similarly, in time-based media, including multipage books, the insertion and distribution of space across time affects perception and pacing.

The ability to create and evaluate effective figure/ground tension is an essential skill for graphic designers. Train your eye to carve out white space as you compose with forms. Learn to massage the positive and negative areas as you adjust the scale of images and typography. Look at the shapes each element makes and see if the edges frame a void that is equally appealing. Notice how as the value of a text block becomes darker, its shape becomes more defined when composed with other elements.

Recognizing the potency of the ground, designers strive to reveal its constructive necessity. Working with figure/ground relationships gives designers the power to create—and destroy—form.

Figure Sky These photographs use urban buildings to frame letterforms. The empty sky becomes the dominant figure, and the buildings become the background that makes them visible. Lisa Rienermann, University of Essen, Germany.

Stable

Reversible

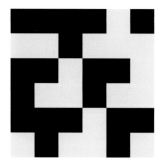

Ambiguous

Stable, Reversible, Ambiguous

A stable figure/ground relationship exists when a form or figure stands clearly apart from its background. Most photography functions according to this principle, where someone or something is featured within a setting.

Reversible figure/ground occurs when positive and negative elements attract our attention equally and alternately, coming forward, then receding, as our eye perceives one first as dominant and next as subordinate. Reversible figure ground motifs can be seen in the ceramics, weaving, and crafts of cultures around the globe.

Images and compositions featuring ambiguous figure/ground challenge the viewer to find a focal point. Figure is enmeshed with ground, carrying the viewer's eye in and around the surface with no discernable assignment of dominance. The Cubist paintings of Picasso mobilize this ambiguity.

Interwoven Space

Designers, illustrators, and photographers often play with figure/ground relationships to add interest and intrigue to their work. Unlike conventional depictions where subjects are centered and framed against a background, active figure/ground conditions churn and interweave form and space, creating tension and ambiguity.

Form and Counterform Sculpture—like buildings in a landscape—displaces space, creating an active interplay between the form and void around it. Here, the distilled shapes and taut tension pay homage to Henry Moore, with whom this artist studied in the 1930s. Reuben Kramer, 1937. Photographed by Dan Meyers.

ZAPRASZAMY DO KIN

SHOOTING DOGS

Michael Caton-Jones

WWW.VIVARTO.PL

Figure Inside of Figure This poster reveals its subject at second glance. One head takes form as the void inside the other. The tension between figure and ground acquires an ominous energy. Joanna Górska and Jerzy Skakun, Homework.

Letterform Abstraction In this introduction
to letterform anatomy, students examined
the forms and counterforms of the alphabet
in many font variations, eventually isolating
just enough of each letter to hint at its
identity. Each student sought to strike a
balance between positive and negative space.
Typography I. Jennifer Cole Phillips, faculty.

Optical Interplay This mark for Vanderbilt University employs a strong contrast between rigid form and organic counterform. The elegant oak leaf alternately sinks back, allowing the letterform to read, and comes forward, connoting growth, strength, and beauty. Malcolm Grear, Malcolm Grear Designers.

Figure/Ground Battalion These marching positive and negative arrows commingle and break away from the pack. The dynamic use of scale, direction, rhythm, and color ushers the viewer's eye in and around the composition. Superforms take shape out of the crowd. Yong Seuk Lee, MFA Studio.

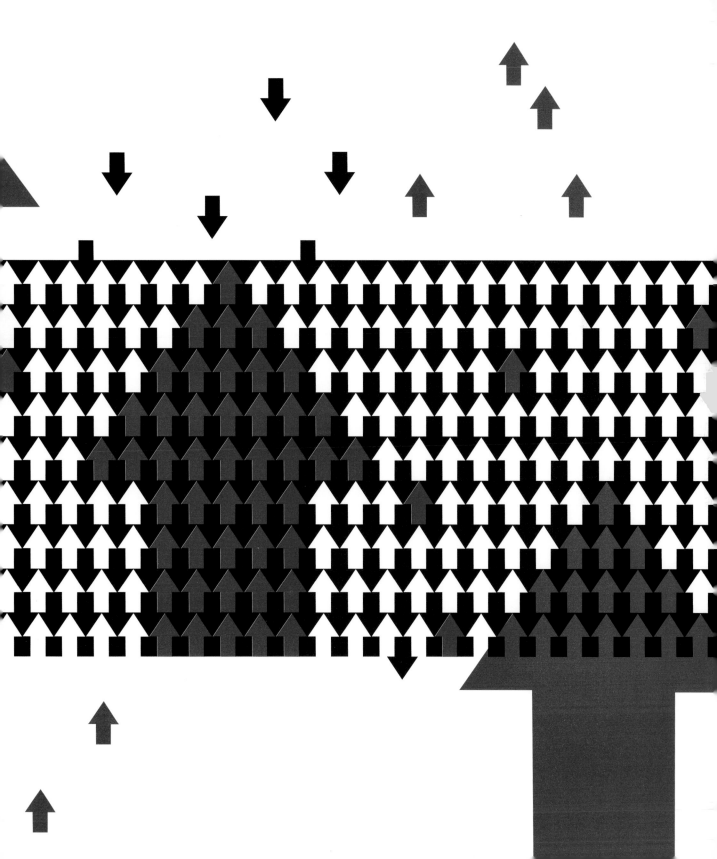

Photo Letter Mesh In this abstract study of type and texture, black and white letterforms are skillfully interwoven with granular, high-contrast imagery, creating an ambiguous figure/ground condition. Jeremy Botts, MFA Studio.

Contrast and Composition. In this project, students explored principles of visual contrast, homing in on letterform details to illuminate unique anatomical and stylistic features. Each study focuses on one pair of contrasting letterforms, which the designer could crop, combine, repeat, rotate, enlarge, and reduce. The final designs celebrate formal differences as well as distribute positive and negative space into fluid, balanced compositions. Typography I. Jennifer Cole Phillips, faculty.

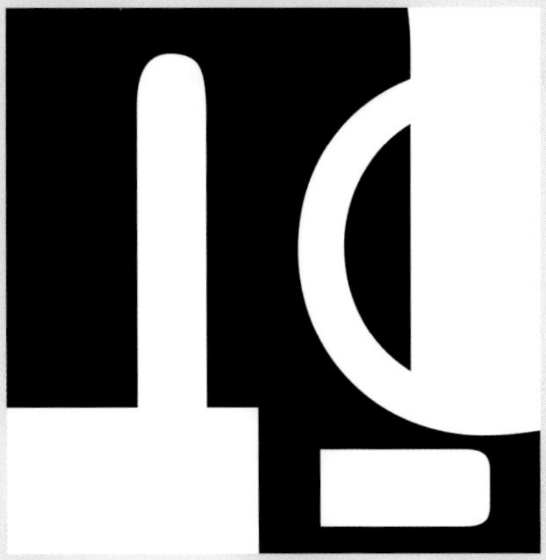

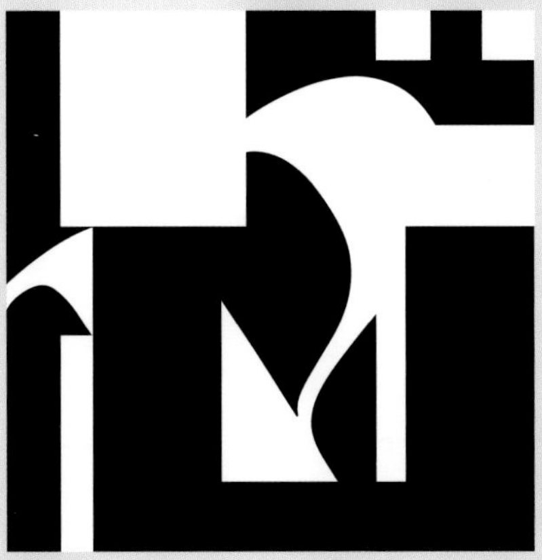

Zey Akay
Anna Eshelman
HyunSoo Lim

Lindsay Petrick
Elizabeth Tipson
Lindsay Petrick

The Guggenheim Museum

Artful Reduction A minimal stack of carefully shaped forms, in concert with exacting intervals of spaces, instantly evokes this sculptural landmark. Malcolm Grear, Malcolm Grear Designers.

Capturing Tension Aaron Siskind (1903–1991), known for his profound contribution to abstract expressionist photography, was a master of figure/ground relationships. *Chicago 30, 1949,* above, challenges the viewer to choose figure or ground as the tension between black and white is continually shifting. ©Aaron Siskind Foundation. Image courtesy of Robert Mann Gallery.

No Entry These crudely punched letters are readable against the sky and sea, whose contrasting value lights up the message. Jayme Odgers.

Counter Hand The simple device of cut white paper held against a contrasting ground defines the alphabet with quirky style and spatial depth. FWIS Design.

Seeing Jesus Simple stitches spell out
a series of letters, which take form as
the viewer's eye allows the background
to move forward. The light stitches
become counterforms for the dark letters.
Needlepoint: Ralph Emerson Pierce
(1912–1992). Photograph: Jeremy Botts,
MFA Studio.

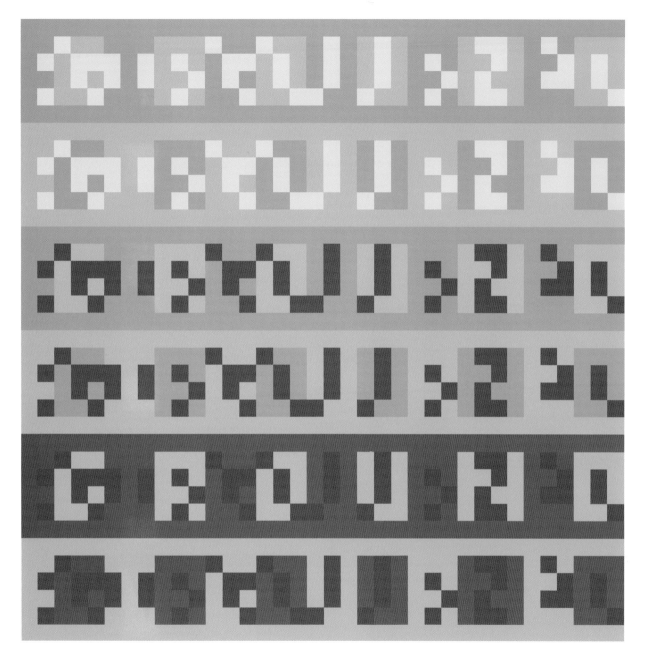

Inspired by Jesus The designer has interwoven the words "figure" and "ground" across each horizontal band. One word serves as the background or frame for the other, forcing the eye to shuttle between two conflicting readings. This complex study was inspired by the needlework at left. Jeremy Botts, MFA Studio.

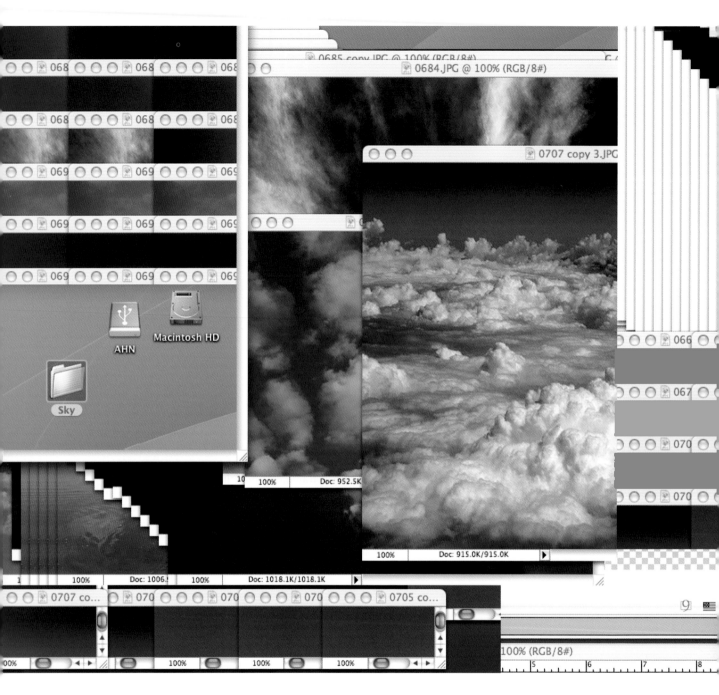

Interface Overload Graphic interfaces are a constant presence throughout the design process. Here, the interface itself—and its excessive accumulation of windows—becomes a design object. Yeohyun Ahn, MFA Studio.

Framing

[The frame] disappears, buries itself, melts away at the moment it deploys its greatest energy. **The frame is in no way a background…but neither is its thickness as margin a figure. Or at least it is a figure which comes away of its own accord.** Jacques Derrida

Frames are everywhere. A picture frame sets off a work of art from its surroundings, bringing attention to the work and lifting it apart from its setting. Shelves, pedestals, and vitrines provide stages for displaying objects. A saucer frames a tea cup, and a place mat outlines the pieces of a table setting.

Modern designers often seek to eliminate frames. A minimalist interior avoids moldings around doors or woodwork where walls meet the floor, exposing edge-to-edge relationships. The full-bleed photography of a sleek magazine layout eliminates the protective, formal zone of the white margin, allowing the image to explode off the page and into reality.

In politics, "framing" refers to explaining an issue in terms that will influence how people interpret it. The caption of a picture is a frame that guides its interpretation. A billboard is framed by a landscape, and a product is framed by its retail setting. Boundaries and fences mark the frames of private property.

Cropping, borders, margins, and captions are key resources of graphic design. Whether emphasized or erased, frames affect how we perceive information.

Frames create the conditions for understanding an image or object. The philosopher Jacques Derrida defined framing as a structure that is both present and absent.[1] The frame is subservient to the content it surrounds, disappearing as we focus on the image or object on view, and yet the frame shapes our understanding of that content. Frames are part of the fundamental architecture of graphic design. Indeed, framing is one of the most persistent, unavoidable, and infinitely variable acts performed by the graphic designer.

An interface is a kind of frame. The buttons on a television set, the index of a book, or the toolbars of a software application exist outside the central purpose of the product, yet they are essential to our understanding of it. A hammer with no handle or a cell phone with no controls is useless.

Consider the ubiquity of interfaces in the design process. The physical box of the computer screen provides a constant frame for the act of designing, while the digital desktop is edged with controls and littered with icons. Numerous windows compete for our attention, each framed by borders and buttons.

A well-designed interface is both visible and invisible, escaping attention when not needed while shifting into focus on demand. Once learned, interfaces disappear from view, becoming second nature.

Experimental design often exposes or dramatizes the interface: a page number or a field of white space might become a pronounced visual element, or a navigation panel might assume an unusual shape or position. By pushing the frame into the foreground, such acts provoke the discovery of new ideas.

This chapter shows how the meaning and impact of an image or text changes depending on how it is bordered or cropped. Frames typically serve to contain an image, marking it off from its background in order to make it more visible. Framing can also penetrate the image, rendering it open and permeable rather than stable and contained. A frame can divide an image from its background, but it can also serve as a transition from inside to outside, figure to ground.

1. Jacques Derrida, *The Truth in Painting*, trans. Geoff Bennington and Ian McLeod (Chicago: University of Chicago Press, 1987).

Camera Frames

The mechanical eye of the camera cuts up the field of vision in a way that the natural eye does not. Every time you snap a picture with a camera, you make a frame. In contrast, the eye is in constant motion, focusing and refocusing on diverse stimuli in the environment.

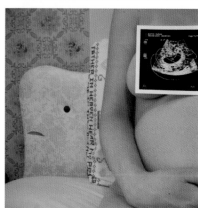

Frames Inside of Frames Frames exist throughout the environment. The photographs shown here use the tool of the camera to create not only the outer frame of the shot, but to discover inner frames as well. Sarah Joy Jordahl Verville, MFA Studio.

Framing and Reframing Here, the artist rephotographed pictures collected from the history and future of his own family in environments that are endowed with both historic and contemporary detail. Jeremy Botts, MFA Studio. Corinne Botz, faculty.

Cropping

By cropping a photograph or illustration, the designer redraws its borders and alters its shape, changing the scale of its elements in relation to the overall picture. A vertical image can become a square, a circle, or a narrow ribbon, acquiring new proportions. By closing in on a detail, cropping can change the focus of a picture, giving it new meaning and emphasis.

By cropping a picture, the designer can discover new images inside it. Experiment with cropping by laying two L-shaped pieces of paper over an image, or look at the picture through a window cut from a piece of paper. Working digitally, move an image around inside the picture frame in a page-layout program, changing its scale, position, and orientation.

New Frame, New Meaning The way an image is cropped can change its meaning completely. Yong Seuk Lee, MFA Studio.

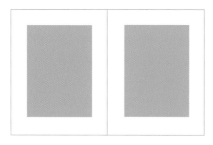

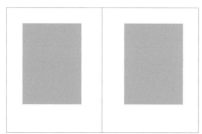

Margin A margin creates a protective zone around an image, presenting it as an object on a stage, a figure against a ground. Margins can be thick or thin, symmetrical or asymmetrical. A wider margin can add formality to the image it frames.

Margins and Bleeds

Margins affect the way we perceive content by providing open spaces around texts and images. Wider margins can emphasize a picture or a field of text as an object, calling our attention to it. Narrower margins can make the content seem larger than life, bursting at its own seams.

Margins provide a protective frame around the contents of a publication. They also provide space for information such as page numbers and running heads. A deep margin can accommodate illustrations, captions, headings, and other information.

Full Bleed An image "bleeds" when it runs off the edges of a page. The ground disappears, and the image seems larger and more active.

Partial Bleed An image can bleed off one, two, or three sides. Here, the bottom margin provides a partial border, yet the photograph still has a larger-than-life quality.

Bleeds The picture above is reproduced at the same scale in each instance, but its intimacy and impact change as it takes over more or less of the surrounding page.

Louise **That sounds stringent. During Modernism we insisted on modesty because we believed it would help us penetrate further and further into the essence of things. The art of omission.**

Hella **It's more than that. You consciously avoid designing new forms, but you add a new dimension, a different function or a different story. That's like what I do. When I get a commission from Maharam, I don't rush to my drawing board to design a snazzy new pattern. I pore through the archives, use existing patterns, and add a new concept to them.**

Louise **You confront tradition with the banality of camping gear.**

Hella **To that you can add that I confront the beauty of tradition with the beauty of the banal.**

Using Margins and Bleeds Designed by COMA, this book about the Dutch product designer Hella Jongerius uses margins, bleeds, rules, and other framing devices in distinctive ways. The photographs bleed off the left and right edges of each page, while the top and bottom margins are kept clear as an open territory that sometimes includes text and additional pictures. Tightly spaced together, the pictures create a strong horizontal movement, like a strip of film marching through the center of the book. Countering this horizontal motion are gold boxes printed on top of the pictures. Whereas boxes traditionally serve to neatly enclose an area, these boxes are open at the top, and their shape doesn't match the pictures underneath. The designers have thus used many of the standard components of book design in an unconventional way. Cornelia Blatter and Marcel Hermans, COMA. *Hella Jongerius*, 2003. Photographers: Joke Robaard with Maarten Theuwkens.

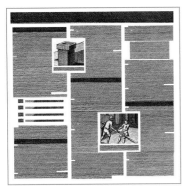

Shannon Snyder

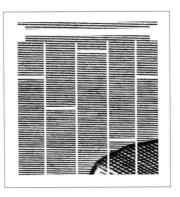

Jessica Alvarado

Melanie M. Rodgers

Lindsay Olson

Using Images Typographically How can an image be arranged, like type, into words, lines, columns, and grids? This exercise invited designers to think abstractly about both image and type. Each designer created a new visual "text" by mining lines, shapes, and textures from a larger picture. Typography is experienced in terms of blocks of graphic tone and texture that are framed by the margins and gutters of the page. Different densities of texture suggest hierarchies of contrasting typefaces. Headlines, captions, quotations, lists, illustrations, and other material take shape in relation to bodies of running text. Advanced Design Workshop, York College. Ellen Lupton, visiting faculty.

The exercises on this spread incorporate a high-resolution scan of an original eighteenth-century engraving from Denis Diderot's *Encyclopedia*. Shown here is the full image.

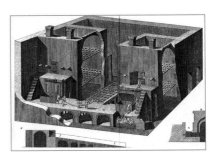

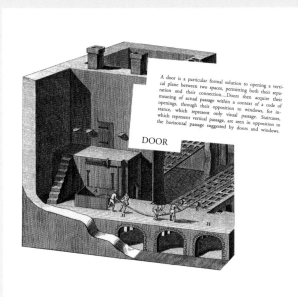

Luke Williams

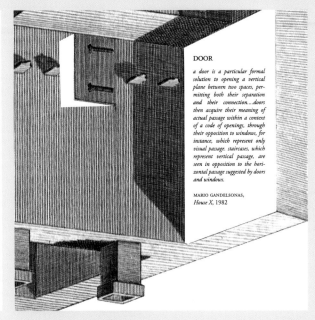

Jessica Neil

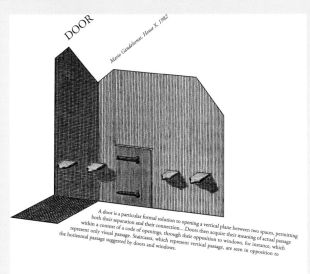

Jonnie Hallman

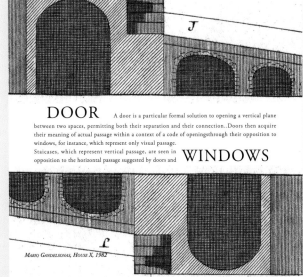

Lindsey Sherman

Framing Text and Image In this project, designers edited, framed, and cropped a picture in relation to a passage of text. The challenge was to make the text an equal player in the final composition, not a mere caption or footnote to the picture.

Designers approached the image abstractly as well as figuratively. Is the picture flat or three-dimensional? How does it look upside down? Designers edited the image by blocking out parts of it, changing the shape of the frame, or blowing up a detail.

They found lines, shapes, and planes within the picture that suggested ways to position and align the text. The goal was to integrate the text with the image without letting the text disappear. Typography I. Ellen Lupton, faculty.

EMPTY SPACE AVAILABLE. COMMERCIAL LEASE, 10,000 SQUARE FT.

Framing Image and Text

An image seen alone, without any words, is open to interpretation. Adding text to a picture changes its meaning. Written language becomes a frame for the image, shaping the viewer's understanding of it both through the content of the words and the style and placement of the typography. Likewise, pictures can change the meaning of a text.

Text and image combine in endless ways. Text can be subordinate or dominant to a picture; it can be large or small, inside or outside, opaque or transparent, legible or obscure. Text can respect or ignore the borders of an image.

From Caption to Headline When a large-scale word replaces an ordinary caption, the message changes. What is empty? The sky, the store, or the larger social reality suggested by the landscape?

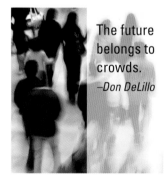

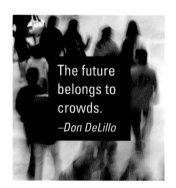

Text Over Image Putting type on top of a high-contrast image poses legibility conflicts. Boxes, bars, and transparent color fields are some of the ways designers deal with the problem of separating text from image.

Framing Image and Text Pages and covers from the Dutch magazine *Frame,* designed by COMA, combine image and text in diverse ways. The designers rarely use frames as a closed box or border. Images as well as texts are often cut or broken, bleeding off the edge, or slipping behind other elements. Cornelia Blatter and Marcel Hermans, COMA.

Villa Borghese, Rome, 1615. The ornament on this Renaissance palazzo frames the windows, doors, and niches as well as delineates the building's principal volumes and divisions. Architect: Giovanni Vasanzio. Vintage photograph.

Borders

A border is the frontier between inside and outside, marking the edge of a territory. A border naturally appears where an image ends and its background begins.

While many images hold their own edges (a dark picture on a white background), a graphic border can help define an image that lacks an obvious edge (a white background on a white page). A graphic border can emphasize an outer boundary, or it can frame off a section inside an image. Some borders are simple lines; others are detailed and complex. Around the world and across history, people have created elaborate frames, rules, cartouches, and moldings to frame pictures and architectural elements.

Marking Space A frame can mark off a space with just a few points. Territory can be defined from the outside in (as in crop marks for trimming a print), or from the inside out (an x drawn from the center of a space to its four corners).

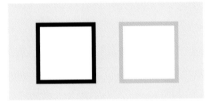

Whether simple or decorative, a border creates a transition between image and background. Against the pale wall of a room, for example, a black picture frame sharply separates a work of art from its surroundings. Alternatively, a frame whose color is close to that of the wall blends the work of art with the room around it. Graphic designers make similar decisions when framing visual elements, sometimes seeking to meld them with their context, and sometimes seeking to set them sharply apart. A frame can serve to either emphasize or downplay its contents.

Border Patrol Frames interact with content in different ways. In the examples shown here, the border sometimes calls attention to the icon, lending it stature; in other instances, the border itself takes over, becoming the dominant form. Robert Lewis, MFA Studio.

PRODUCT OF TRINIDAD & TOBAGO

OVER 65% ALC./VOL.

Hierarchy

Design is the conscious effort to impose a **meaningful order**.

Victor Papanek

Hierarchy is the order of importance within a social group (such as the regiments of an army) or in a body of text (such as the sections and subsections of a book). Hierarchical order exists in nearly everything we know, including the family unit, the workplace, politics, and religion. Indeed, the ranking of order defines who we are as a culture.

Hierarchy is expressed through naming systems: general, colonel, corporal, private, and so on. Hierarchy is also conveyed visually, through variations in scale, value, color, spacing, placement, and other signals. Expressing order is a central task of the graphic designer. Visual hierarchy controls the delivery and impact of a message. Without hierarchy, graphic communication is dull and difficult to navigate.

Like fashion, graphic design cycles through periods of structure and chaos, ornament and austerity. A designer's approach to visual hierarchy reflects his or her personal style, methodology, and training as well as the zeitgeist of the period. Hierarchy can be simple or complex, rigorous or loose, flat or highly articulated. Regardless of approach, hierarchy employs clear marks of separation to signal a change from one level to another. As in music, the ability to articulate variation in tone, pitch, and melody in design requires careful delineation.

In interaction design, menus, texts, and images can be given visual order through placement and consistent styling, but the user often controls the order in which information is accessed. Unlike a linear book, interactive spaces feature multiple links and navigation options that parcel the content according to the user's actions. Cascading Style Sheets (CSS) articulate the structure of a document separately from its presentation so that information can be automatically reconfigured for different output devices, from desktop computer screens to mobile phones, PDAs, kiosks, and more. A different visual hierarchy might be used in each instance.

The average computer desktop supports a complex hierarchy of icons, applications, folders, menus, images, and palettes—empowering users, as never before, to arrange, access, edit, and order vast amounts of information—all managed through a flexible hierarchy controlled and customized by the user.

As technology allows ever greater access to information, the ability of the designer to distill and make sense of the data glut gains increasing value.

Inverted Hierarchy This package design project asks students to redirect a product line to an unexpected audience. This design for cleaning products reorders the hierarchy and voice to spark the interest of young, progressive consumers who may be new to housekeeping. The brand name is subtle and sits back, while the offending soil takes center stage. Oliver Munday, Advancd Design. Jennifer Cole Phillips, faculty.

Basic Typographic Hierarchy

The table of contents of a printed book—especially one with many parts—provides a structural picture of the text to follow. When books are marketed online, the table of contents is often reproduced to allow potential buyers to preview the book. A well-designed table of contents is thus not only functional but also visually exciting and memorable.

The basic function of a table of contents is to help readers locate relevant information and provide an image of how the book is organized. Does the text fall into a few main parts with various subdivisions, or does it consist of numerous small, parallel entries? The designer uses alignment, leading, indents, and type sizes and styles to construct a clear and descriptive hierarchy.

A poorly designed table of contents often employs conflicting and contradictory alignments, redundant numbering systems, and a clutter of graphic elements. Analyzing tables of contents—as well as restaurant menus and commercial catalogs—is a valuable exercise.

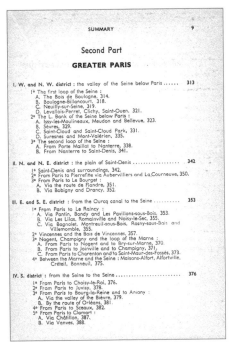

What's Wrong with this Picture?
The function of a table of contents is to list the elements of a book and help readers locate them. In the table of contents shown here, the page numbers are stretched across the page from the chapter titles, and the word "Chapter" has been repeated twenty-four times. *Manners for the Millions*, 1932.

Lost in Paris In this table of contents for a travel guide, the designer has used a muddled mix of centered, justified, and flush-left alignments. The desire to create an overall justified setting dominates the logic of the page—hence the long first lines and rows of dots at the top level of information. The three titling lines at the head of the page are centered (a traditional solution), but the result is awkward in relation to the irregular mass of subheads, which weight the page to the left. The whole affair is further confused by the elaborate system of indents, numerals, and letters used to outline the book's subsections. *Blue Guide to Paris*, 1957.

CONTENTS

Book as Billboard This table of contents serves as a billboard for the book as well as a functional guide to its elements. The designer has approached the spread as a whole, with content stretching across it horizontally. The page numbers are aligned in columns next to the article titles, making it easy for readers to connect content with location. (No old-fashioned leader lines needed!) Chapter numbers aren't necessary because the sequential page numbers are sufficient to indicate the order of the pieces. The book has many contributors, a point made clear through the type styling. Nicholas Blechman, *Empire,* 2004.

Think with the Senses
Feel with the Mind.
Art in the Present Tense
Venice Biennale
52nd International Art Exhibition
10 June – 21 November
National and Regional Pavilions
and Presentations.
Parallel Exhibitions and Projects

No hierarchy

Think with the Senses
Feel with the Mind.
Art in the Present Tense
Venice Biennale
52nd International Art Exhibition
10 June – 21 November
National and Regional Pavilions
and Presentations.
Parallel Exhibitions and Projects

Contrasting weight

Think with the Senses
Feel with the Mind.
Art in the Present Tense
Venice Biennale
52nd International Art Exhibition
10 June – 21 November
National and Regional Pavilions
and Presentations.
Parallel Exhibitions and Projects

Contrasting color

Think with the Senses
Feel with the Mind.
Art in the Present Tense
Venice Biennale
52nd International Art Exhibition
10 June – 21 November
National and Regional Pavilions
and Presentations.
Parallel Exhibitions and Projects

Alignment

Think with the Senses
Feel with the Mind.
Art in the Present Tense

Venice Biennale

52nd International Art Exhibition
10 June – 21 November
National and Regional Pavilions
and Presentations.
Parallel Exhibitions and Projects

Spatial intervals

Think with the Senses
Feel with the Mind.
Art in the Present Tense

VENICE BIENNALE

52nd International Art Exhibition
10 June – 21 November

National and Regional Pavilions
and Presentations.
Parallel Exhibitions and Projects

Uppercase and spatial intervals

Think with the Senses
Feel with the Mind.
Art in the Present Tense

Venice Biennale

52nd International Art Exhibition
10 June – 21 November

National and Regional Pavilions
and Presentations.
Parallel Exhibitions and Projects

Weight, color, space, alignment

Think with the Senses
Feel with the Mind.
Art in the Present Tense

Venice Biennale

52nd International Art Exhibition
10 June – 21 November

National and Regional Pavilions
and Presentations.
Parallel Exhibitions and Projects

Scale, space, alignment

Think with the Senses
Feel with the Mind.
Art in the Present Tense

Venice Biennale

52nd International Art Exhibition
10 June – 21 November

National and Regional Pavilions
and Presentations.
Parallel Exhibitions and Projects

Italic, scale, color, alignment

Hierarchy 101 A classic exercise is to work
with a basic chunk of information and explore
numerous simple variations, using just
one type family. The parts of a typographic
hierarchy can be signaled with one or more
cues: line break, type style, type size, rules,
and so on.

```
void setup()
{
        size(200, 200);
        frameRate(12);
        sx = width;
        sy = height;
        world = new int[sx][sy][2];
        stroke(255);

                for (int i = 0; i < sx * sy * density; i++)
                        {
                          world[(int)random(sx)][(int)random(sy)][1] = 1;
                        }
}

void draw()
{
        background(0);

        for (int x = 0; x < sx; x=x+1)
                {
                for (int y = 0; y < sy; y=y+1)
                        {
                                if ((world[x][y][1] == 1) || (world[x][y][1] == 0 &&
world[x][y][0] == 1))
                                        {
                                        world[x][y][0] = 1;
                                        point(x, y);
                                        }
                                if (world[x][y][1] == -1)
                                        {
                                        world[x][y][0] = 0;
                                        }
                                        world[x][y][1] = 0;
                        }
                }

        for (int x = 0; x < sx; x=x+1)
                {
                for (int y = 0; y < sy; y=y+1)
                        {
                        int count = neighbors(x, y);

                        if (count == 3 && world[x][y][0] == 0)
                                {
                                world[x][y][1] = 1;
                                }
                        if ((count < 2 || count > 3) && world[x][y][0] == 1)
                                {
                                world[x][y][1] = -1;
                                }
                        }
                }
}

int neighbors(int x, int y)
{
        return world[(x + 1) % sx][y][0] +
        world[x][(y + 1) % sy][0] +
        world[(x + sx - 1) % sx][y][0] +
        world[x][(y + sy - 1) % sy][0] +
        world[(x + 1) % sx][(y + 1) % sy][0] +
        world[(x + sx - 1) % sx][(y + 1) % sy][0] +
        world[(x + sx - 1) % sx][(y + sy - 1) % sy][0] +
        world[(x + 1) % sx][(y + sy - 1) % sy][0];
}
```

```
void setup() { size(200, 200);
frameRate(12); sx = width;sy
= height; world = new
int[sx][sy][2]; stroke(255);for
(int i = 0; i < sx * sy * den-
sity; i++) { world[(int)
random(sx)][(int)random(
sy)][1] = 1; } } void draw()
{ background(0); for (int
x = 0; x < sx; x=x+1) { for
(int y = 0; y < sy; y=y+1)
if ((world[x][y][1] == 1) ||
(world[x][y][1] == 0 &&
world[x][y][0] == 1)) { world
[x][y][0] = 1; point(x, y);
if (world[x][y][1] == -1)
{world[x][y][0] = 0;
world[x][y][1]=0;} } for(int x =
0; x < sx; x=x+1) { for (int
y = 0; y < sy; y=y+1) { int
count = neighbors(x, y); if
(count == 3 && world[x]
[y][0] == 0){ world[x][y][1
= 1; } if ((count < 2 || count
> 3) && world[x][y][0] ==
1){ world[x][y][1] = -1; } }
int neighbors(int x, int y){
return world[(x + 1) % sx]
[y][0] + world[x][(y + 1) %
sy][0] + world[(x + sx - 1)
% sx][y][0] + world[x][(y
+ sy - 1) % sy][0] + world
[(x + 1) % sx][(y + 1) %
sy][0] + world[(x + sx - 1) %
sx][(y + 1) % sy][0] + world[(x
+ sx - 1) % sx][(y + sy
-1) % sy][0] + world[(x + 1)
% sx][(y + sy - 1) % sy][0];
```

Code Hierarchy Computer code is written
with a structural hierarchy; functions,
routines, and subroutines are nested within
each other in a way that determines the
performance of the code. Indents and line
breaks are used to make this hierarchy clear
to the programmer.

Flat Hierarchy The visual hierarchy makes no
difference, however, to the machine. All that
matters from the software's point of view is
the linear order of the code. Although the
visually flat sequence shown here functions
for the computer, it is confusing for the
human programmer. Yeohyun Ahn, MFA
Studio.

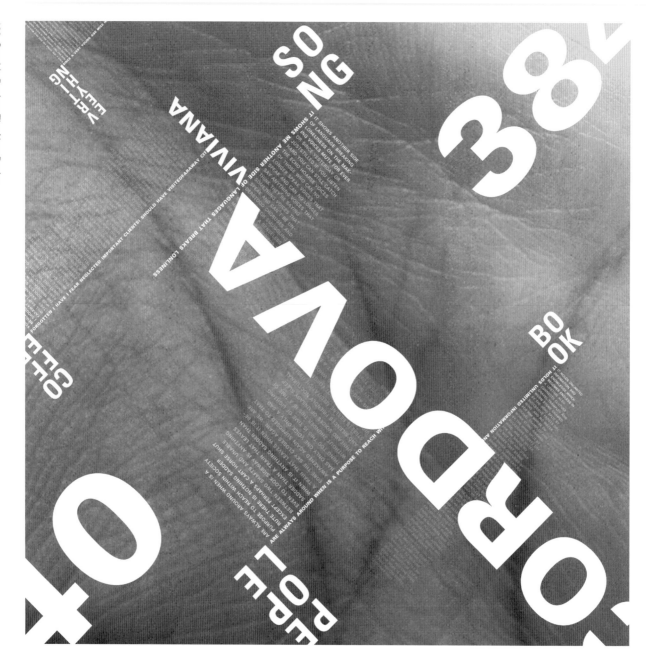

Hierarchy through Contrast The Russian constructivists discovered that the dramatic use of scale, photography, and color imbued their political messages with a powerful and provocative voice. These pioneers used contrast in the size, angle, and value of elements to create hierarchical separation.

This project asked designers to build a hierarchy by combining an image of their hand with a list of autobiographical facts. Elements were restricted to 30 or 45 degree angles; scale, position, color, and transparency were employed to control the transmission of information. Viviana Cordova, MFA Studio.

HyunSoo Lim
Katie MacLachlan

Claire Smalley
Anna Eshelman

Menu of Options Designers use scale, placement, alignment, type style, and other cues to bring visual order to a body of content. Expressing hierarchy is an active, inquisitive process that can yield dynamic visual results. Typography I. Jennifer Cole Phillips, faculty.

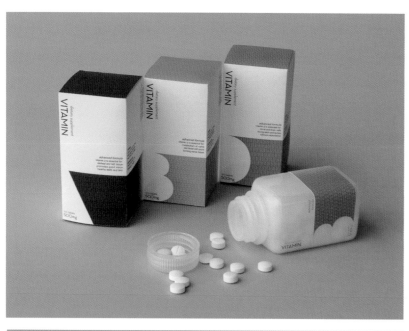

Robert Ferrell

Dimensional Hierarchy

Messages applied to three-dimensional form have the added challenge of legibility across and around planes. Objects sitting in an environment are bathed in shadow and light. Unlike books that can conceal elaborate worlds inside their covers—automatically separated from exterior contexts—environmental messages must interact beyond their boundaries and become either a harmonious counterpart or poignant counterpoint to their neighbors.

Notice in these examples how type, color fields, and graphic elements carry the viewer's eye around the dimensional form, often making a visual if not verbal connection with neighboring packages when stacked side by side or vertically.

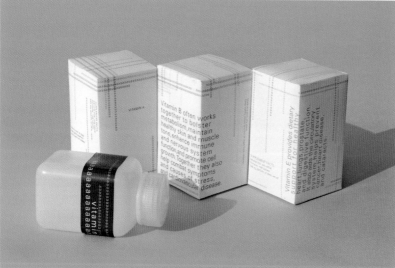

Emily Addis

Typography Across Three Dimensions
A visual hierarchy is often necessary for objects in a series. In these designs for vitamin packaging, students have expressed the identity of the individual product as well as the overall brand. Typography II. Jennifer Cole Phillips, faculty.

Bruce Willen

Unexpected Hierarchy This project takes existing brands and redirects them to unexpected audiences. Here, the designer focuses on a generic food line and reverses the usual order of emphasis by placing the nutrition facts front and center; instead of words, images of the actual product are used to promote what's inside. Advanced Graphic Design. Jennifer Cole Phillips, faculty.

Web Hierarchy In a complex website, numerous systems of hierarchy are at work simultaneously. Here, the navigation consists of a global menu along the right edge as well as a more finely grained index positioned in the main content window.

A "data cloud" uses different sizes of type to automatically represent the frequency with which these tags occur. In many sites, such data clouds change in response to user-added content. The search feature allows users to cut through the hierarchy altogether. William Berry, Cooper-Hewitt, National Design Museum.

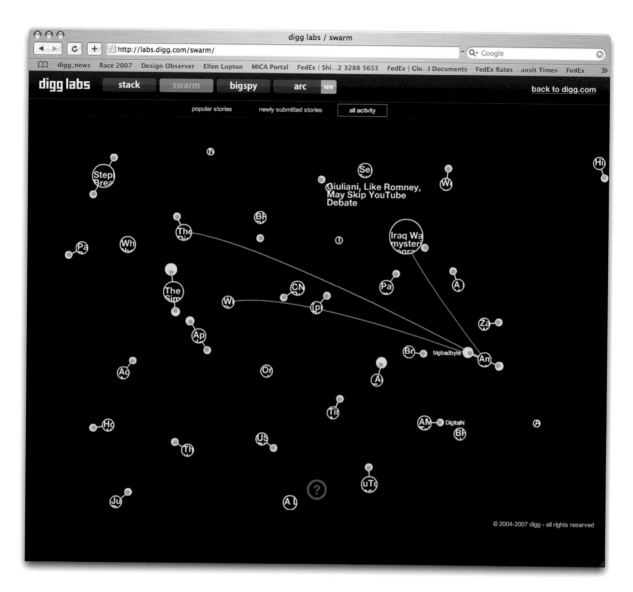

Dynamic Hierarchy This popular web portal displays stories in swarms as authors submit them in real time. The interface feels like a computer game, where trigger-fast selections are needed to engage the content. Elements in the field grow and gain color according to the number of "diggs," reflecting a changing hierarchy. Stamen Design.

Layers

Under cities you always find **other cities**; under churches other churches; and under houses other houses. Pablo Picasso

Layers are simultaneous, over-lapping components of an image or sequence. They are at work in countless media software programs, from Photoshop and Illustrator to audio, video, and animation tools, where multiple layers of image and sound (tracks) unfold in time.

The concept of layers comes from the physical world, and it has a long history in the traditions of mapping and musical notation. Maps and time lines use overlapping layers to associate different levels of data, allowing them to contribute to the whole while maintaining their own identities.

Most printing techniques require that an image be split into layers before it can be reproduced. From ink-jet printing to silkscreen and commercial lithography, each color requires its own plate, film, screen, ink cartridge, or toner drum, depending on the process. Digital technologies automate this process, making it more or less invisible to the designer.

Before the early 1990s, designers created "mechanicals" consisting of precisely aligned layers of paper and acetate. The designer or paste-up artist adhered each element of the page—type, images, blocks of color—to a separate layer, placing any element that touches any other element on its own surface.

This same principle is at work in the digital layers we use today, mobilized in new and powerful ways. The layers feature in Photoshop creates a new layer whenever the user adds text or pastes an image. Each layer can be independently filtered, transformed, masked, or multiplied. Adjustment layers allow global changes such as levels and curves to be revised or discarded at any time. The image file becomes an archaeology of its own making, a stack of elements seen simultaneously in the main window, but represented as a vertical list in the layers palette.

Layers allow the designer to treat the image as a collection of assets, a database of possibilities. Working with a layered file, the designer quickly creates variations of a single design by turning layers on and off. Designers use layered files to generate storyboards for animations and interface elements such as buttons and rollovers.

Although the layered archeology of the printed page or digital file tends to disappear in the final piece, experimental work often uncovers visual possibilities by exposing layers. The Dutch designer Jan van Toorn has used cut-and-paste techniques to create images whose complex surfaces suggest political action and unrest.

Many designers have explored an off-register or misprinted look, seeking rawness and accidental effects by exposing the layers of the printing and production processes. Contemporary graphic artists Ryan McGinness and Joshua Davis create graphic images composed of enormous numbers of layers that overlap in arbitrary, seemingly uncoordinated ways.

Layers, always embedded in the process of mechanical reproduction, have become intuitive and universal. They are crucial to how we both read and produce graphic images today.

Printed Layers Artist and designer Ryan McGinness piles numerous layers on top of each other to yield composite images that celebrate both flatness and depth. Ryan McGinness, *Arab Cadillac Generator*, 2006. Acrylic on wood panel, 48 inches diameter. Collection of Charles Saatchi. Courtesy Deitch Projects, New York. Photo: Tom Powel Imaging, Inc.

Cut and Paste

The cubist painters popularized collage in the early twentieth century. By combining bits of printed paper with their own drawn and painted surfaces, they created an artistic technique that profoundly influenced both design and the fine arts. Like the cubists, modern graphic designers use collage to juxtapose layers of content, yielding surfaces that oscillate between flatness and depth, positive and negative.

The cut-and-paste function used in nearly every software application today refers to the physical process of collage. Each time you copy or delete a picture or phrase and insert it into a new position, you reference the material act of cutting and pasting. The collaged history of an image or a document largely disappears in the final work, and designers often strive to create seamless, invisible transitions between elements. Foregrounding the cut-and-paste process can yield powerful results that indicate the designer's role in shaping meaning.

Mixing Media Published in 1989 to commemorate the Declaration of Human Rights a century earlier, this poster by Jan van Toorn used photomechanical processes to mix handmade and mass-media imagery. Scraps of paper radiate like energy from the central handshake. Jan van Toorn, *La Lutte Continue* (The Fight Continues), 1989.

An Innovative Study

Center | *for* Applied Research

call for collaborations

Phone | 410 225 2383

Maryland Institute College of Art

1300 Mount Royal Avenue | Baltimore, Maryland 21217
410 - 669 - 9200 | www.mica.edu

An Innovative Study

Center | *for* | Applied Research

call for collaborations

www.CenterforAppliedResearch.org

Maryland Institute College of Art

1300 Mount Royal Avenue | Baltimore, Maryland 21217
410 - 669 - 9200 | www.mica.edu

An Innovative Study

Center | *for* Applied Research

call for collaborations

Deadline for Entries | Dec. 14, 2006

Maryland Institute College of Art

1300 Mount Royal Avenue | Baltimore, Maryland 21217
410 - 669 - 9200 | www.mica.edu

Cut, Paste, Tape, Splice These posters originated from hands-on experiments with physical cutting and pasting, which then evolved into digital interpretations. Luke Williams, Graphic Design I. Bernard Canniffe, faculty.

The many-sidedness of human experience is seriously threatened by the common denominator of mass communication. That is why designers who are concerned by the corporate take-over of expression must first allow themselves sufficient room to maneuver for a **dissident attitude** vis-a-vis the normative determination of the media culture. Jan van Toorn

Combine and Contrast

In the project shown here, students were given two digital photographs and the quotation above by the legendary Dutch designer Jan van Toorn. The photographs depict two idealized visions of femininity: an industrially produced garden statue of the Madonna and a department-store mannequin. The quote by van Toorn calls on designers to manipulate creatively the global language of standardized images.

As part of the design process, students were asked to study van Toorn's work and consider the ways he splices and overlaps words and images. Seeking to express his own "dissident attitude" toward mass media, van Toorn generates surprise and tension by presenting fragments of words and images, working primarily with hands-on cut-and-paste techniques and photomechanical processes. He often cuts or places images at an angle to indicate informality and change. Graphic Design II. Jan van Toorn, visiting faculty.

Cut, Crop, Paste To create this museum poster, the Dutch designer Jan van Toorn cut and pasted elements, assembling them for photomechanical reproduction. Jan van Toorn. *Je ne cherche pas, je trouve* (I do not search, I find). Cultural centre De Beyerd, Breda, Netherlands, 1985.

Claire Smalley
Grey Haas
Sisi Recht

Lindsey Sherman
Katie Evans
Marleen Kuijf

Giulia Marconi
Jonnie Hallman
Dani Bradford

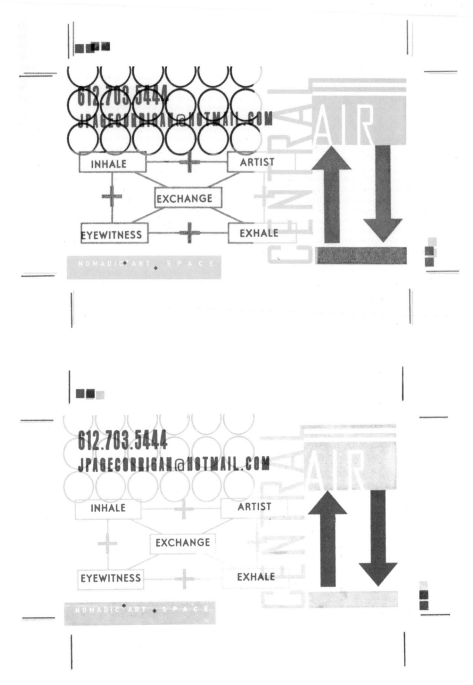

Printed Layers Nearly every color printing process uses layers of ink, but the layers are usually compiled to create the appearance of a seamless, singular surface. The screen prints above use overlapping and misaligned layers of ink to call attention to the structure of the surface. John P. Corrigan, MFA Studio.

Makeready To conserve materials, printers reuse old press sheets while getting their presses up to speed, testing ink flow and position before pulling their final prints. Called "makereadies," these layered surfaces are full of beautiful accidental effects, as seen in this screen-printed makeready. Paul Sahre and David Plunkert.

SEPTEMBER 27 THRU OCTOBER 27   DIRECTED BY SUSAN KRAMER

BALTIMORE PREMIERE!

A PLAY BY: JON KLEIN

THE

BY WALLACE SHAWN

PERFORMED BY: NEAL HEMPHILL

REVERSE

NE'S POINT CORNER THEATRE

BALTIMORE PREMIERE!
A PLAY BY KLEIN
DIRECTED BY SUSAN KRAMER
SEPTEMBER 27 THRU OCTOBER 27

April Osmanof

Mixing Layers The two compositions shown here were each made from the same set of digital images, layered together to create different designs. Various relationships are built by changing the scale, position, color, or transparency of elements. MFA Studio. Source images: Jason Okutake, photography; Robert Lewis, flying fish.

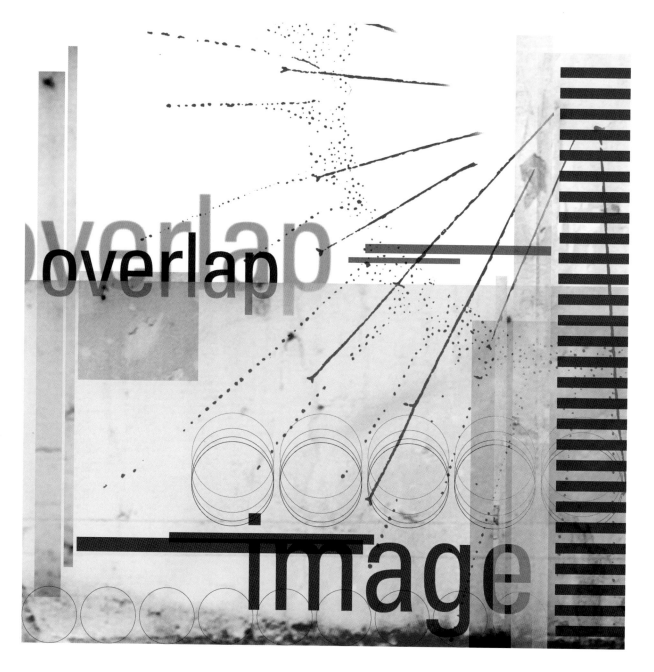

HyunSoo Lim

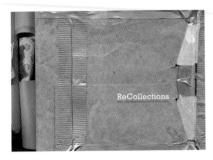

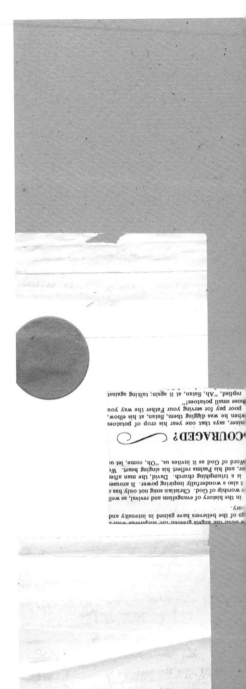

Spatial Layers

Layered objects and surfaces exist throughout the visual environment. On the walls of an old farmhouse, layers—from wallpaper and works of art to ordinary electrical outlets—accumulate over time.

By layering scans of flat surfaces with photographs of three-dimensional space, the designer of the book shown here has created an interplay between surface and depth. Overlapping forms and optical alignments produce surprising spatial relationships. Even the shallow space of a scanned surface can reveal an element of depth through its texture, folds, transparency, and imperfections. The surface thus conveys a sense of time and history.

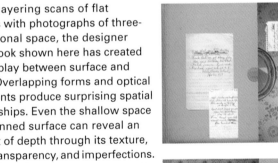

Collage with Depth The designer has combined a stack of poems written by his grandfather with photographs of the wallpaper in his farmhouse. The pages invite the viewer to read the texts against a complex spatial surface.
Jeremy Botts, MFA Studio. Charles Bonner, handwritten poems.

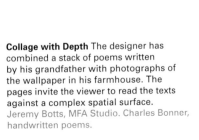

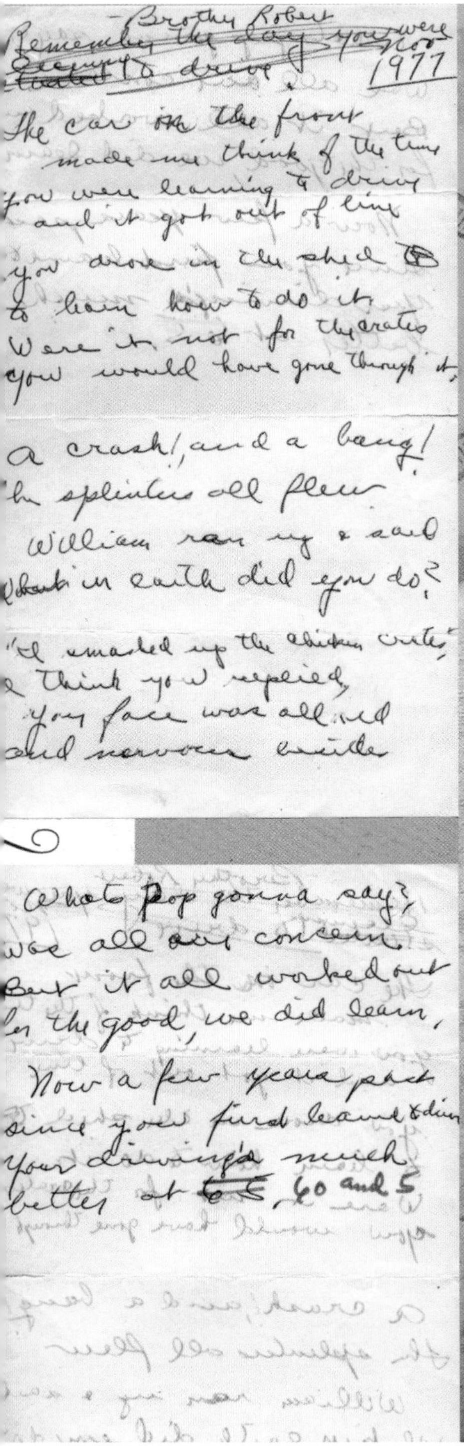

—Brother Robert
Remember the day you were
learning to drive! 1977

The car in the front
made me think of the time
you were learning to drive
and it got out of line
you drove in the shed
to learn how to do it,
Were it not for the crates
you would have gone through it,

a crash! and a bang!
th splinters all flew
William ran up & said
What in earth did you do?

"I smashed up the chicken crates,
I think you replied,
Your face was all red
and nervous smile

What's pop gonna say?
was all our concern.
But it all worked out
for the good, we did learn,

Now a few years past
since you furd learned to drive
Your driving's much
better at 60 and 5

It's soon He's coming back again
To take His bride away
"even Bugs get on the hay"

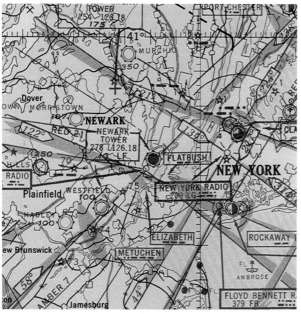

Data Layers: Static This map uses point, line, plane, and color to indicate geographic borders, topographical features, towns and cities, and points of interest, as well as radio systems used by pilots in the air. The purple lines indicating radio signals read as a separate layer. Aeronautical map, 1946.

Data Layers

Maps compress various types of information—topography, water systems, roadways, cities, geographic borders, and so on—onto a single surface. Map designers use color, line, texture, symbols, icons, and typography to create different levels of information, allowing users to read levels independently (for example, learning what roads connect two destinations) as well as perceiving connections between levels (will the journey be mountainous or flat?).

Sophisticated map-making tools are now accessible to designers and general practitioners as well as to professional cartographers. Google Earth enables users to build personalized maps using satellite photography of the Earth's surface. The ability to layer information over a base image is a central feature of this immensely powerful yet widely available tool.

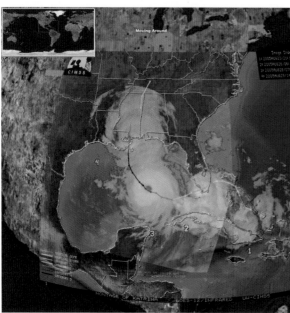

Data Layers: Dynamic An image of Hurricane Katrina has been layered over a satellite photograph of Earth. The end user of a Google Earth overlay can manipulate its transparency in order to control the degree of separation between the added layer and the ground image. Storm: University of Wisconsin, Madison Cooperative Institute for Meteorogical Satellite Studies, 2005. Composite: Jack Gondela.

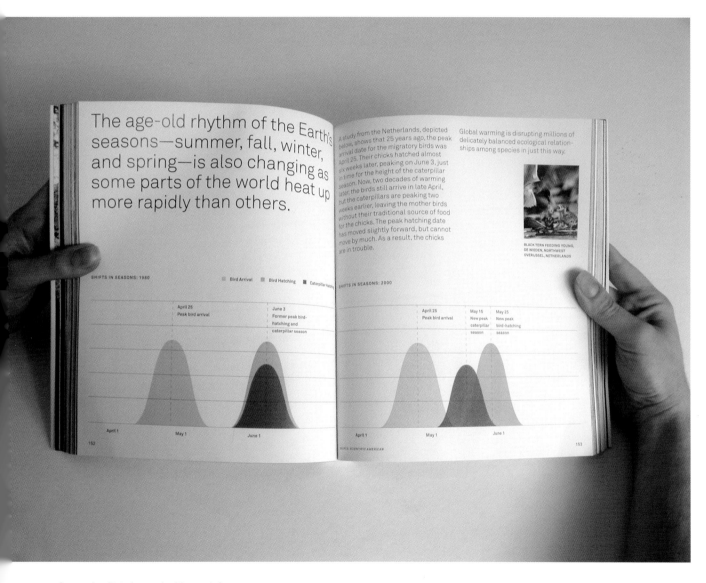

Comparing Data Layers In this graph from Al Gore's book *An Inconvenient Truth,* the designers have used color and transparency to make it easy for readers to compare two sets of data. The graphs show how climate change is affecting the life cycle of animals and their food supplies. Alicia Cheng, Stephanie Church, and Lisa Maione, MGMT Design, *An Inconvenient Truth,* 2006.

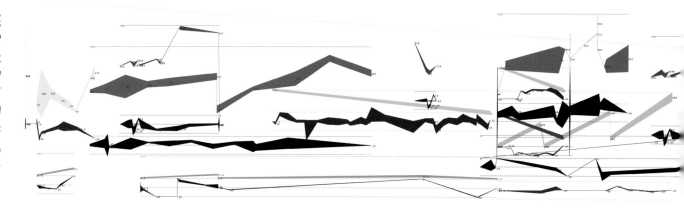

Temporal Layers

In musical notation, the notes for each instrument in a symphony or for each voice in a chorus appear on parallel staffs. The graphic timelines used in audio, video, and animation software follow this intuitive convention, using simultaneous tracks to create composite layers of image and sound.

In soap operas and television dramas, parallel threads unfold alongside each other and converge at key moments in the story. The split screens, inset panels, and text feeds commonly seen in news programming allow several visual tracks to play simultaneously.

From musical notation and computer interfaces to narrative plot lines, parallel linear tracks (layers in time) are a crucial means for describing simultaneous events.

Musical Notation This score shows the notes played by four different musicians simultaneously (first violin, second violin, viola, and cello). Each staff represents a separate instrument. Ludwig van Beethoven, musical score, *String Quartet No. 2 in G Major*, 1799.

Interactive Notation Digital composer Hans-Christoph Steiner has devised his own graphic notation system to show how to manipulate digital samples. Time flows from left to right. Each color represents a sample.

Each sample controller has two arrays: the brighter, bigger one on top controls sample playback, and a smaller, darker one at the bottom controls amp and pan. The lowest point of the sample array is the beginning

of the sample, the highest is the end, and the height of the array is how much and what part of the sample to play, starting at that point in time. Hans-Christoph Steiner, interactive musical score, *Solitude*, 2004.

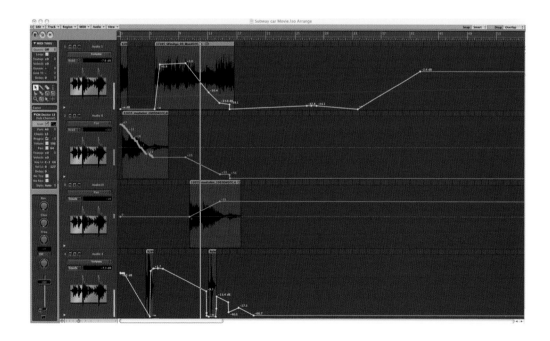

Audio Software Applications for editing digital audio tracks employ complex and varied graphics. Here, each track is represented by a separate timeline. The yellow lines indicate volume, and the green lines show panning left to right. Audio composed by Jason Okutake, MFA Studio. Software: Apple Logic Pro Audio.

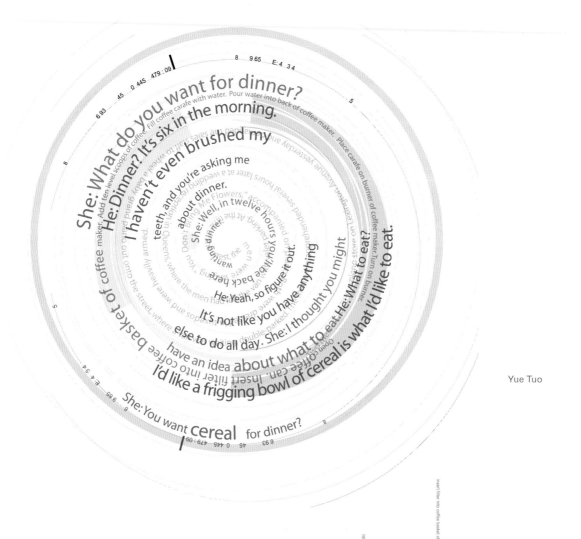

Yue Tuo

Typographic Layers In everyday life as well as in films and animations, multiple stories can unfold simultaneously. A person can talk on the phone while folding the laundry and hearing a song in the background. In films, characters often carry on a conversation while performing an action.

This typographic exercise presents three narratives taking place during a two-minute period: a news story broadcast on a radio, a conversation between a married couple, and the preparation of a pot of coffee. Typography, icons, lines, and other elements are used to present the three narratives within a shared space. The end result can be obvious or poetic. Whether the final piece is an easy-to-follow transcription or a painterly depiction, it is made up of narrative elements that define distinct layers or visual channels. Graphic Design MFA Studio.

Two men broke into a piano store on Lexington Avenue yesterday and demanded the sales staff to wheel a baby grand piano out onto the street, where a van was waiting, double-parked. The men were apprehended several hours later at a wedding reception in Queens, where the men had left the van with valet parking. At the time of the arrest, the men were singing "You Don't Bring Me Flowers.", accompanied on piano. Both were dressed in tuxedos and were heavily armed.

Yong Seuk Lee

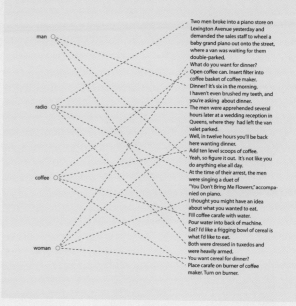

Robert Lewis

Two men broke into a piano store on Lexington Avenue yesterday and demanded the | OPEN COFFEE CAN.

SHE: WHAT DO YOU WANT FOR DINNER?

sales staff to wheel a baby grand piano out onto | INSERT FILTER INTO COFFEE BASKET OF COFFEE MAKER.

HE: DINNER? I HAVEN'T EVEN BRUSHED MY TEETH, AND YOU'RE ASKING ME ABOUT DINNER.

the street, where a van was waiting, double parked. The men were | ADD TEN LEVEL SCOOPS OF COFFEE.

SHE: WELL, IN TWELVE HOURS YOU'LL BE BACK HERE WANTING DINNER.

apprehended several hours later at a wedding reception inQueens, | FILL COFFEE CARAFE WITH WATER.

HE: YEAH, SO FIGURE IT OUT. IT'S NOT LIKE YOU HAVE ANYTHING ELSE TO DO ALL DAY.

where the men had left the van with valet parking. At the | POUR WATER INTO BACK OF COFFEE MAKER.

SHE: I THOUGHT YOU MIGHT HAVE AN IDEA ABOUT WHAT TO EAT.

time of the arrest, the men were singing "you don't bring | PLACE CARAFE ON BURNER OF COFFEE MAKER.

HE: WHAT TO EAT? I'D LIKE A FRIGGING BOWL OF CEREAL IS WHAT I'D LIKE TO EAT.

me flowers," accompanied on piano. Both were dressed in tuxedos and were heavily armed. | TURN ON BURNER.

SHE: YOU WANT CEREAL FOR DINNER?

April Osmanof

Two men broke into a piano store on Lexington Avenue yesterday and demanded the sales staff to wheel a baby grand piano out onto the street, where a van was waiting for them double-parked.
What do you want for dinner?
Open coffee can. Insert filter into coffee basket of coffee maker.
Dinner? It's six in the morning.
I haven't even brushed my teeth, and you're asking about dinner.
The men were apprehended several hours later at a wedding reception in Queens, where they had left the van valet parked.
Well, in twelve hours you'll be back here wanting dinner.
Add ten level scoops of coffee.
Yeah, so figure it out. It's not like you do anything else all day.
At the time of their arrest, the men were singing a duet of "You Don't Bring Me Flowers," accompanied on piano.
I thought you might have an idea about what you wanted to eat.
Fill coffee carafe with water.
Pour water into back of machine.
Eat? I'd like a frigging bowl of cereal is what I'd like to eat.
Both were dressed in tuxedos and were heavily armed.
You want cereal for dinner?
Place carafe on burner of coffee maker. Turn on burner.

HyunSoo Lim

what do you want for dinner? **dinner?** It's **six in the morning.**

I haven't even brushed my teeth, and you're asking me about

dinner. Well, in twelve hours you'll be back here wanting dinner. **Yeah, so figure it out.**

It's **not like you** have anything else to do all day. **I thought you might**

have an idea about what to eat. **What to eat? I'd like a frigging bowl of creral is what I'd**

like to eat. You want **cereal for dinner?**

Visakh Menon

Two men broke into a She: what do you want for dinner? Open coffee can. Insert filter into coffee basket of coffee maker. He: Dinner? Its six in the morning. I haven't even brushed my teeth, and you're asking me about dinner. She: Well, in twelve hours you'll be back here wanting dinner, piano store on Lexington Avenue yesterday and demanded the sales staff to wheel a baby grand piano out onto the street. Add ten level scoops of coffee. where a van was waiting double-parked. The men were apprehended several hours later at a wedding reception in Queens. He: Yeah, so figure it out. Its not like you have anything else to do all day. She: I thought you might have an idea about what to eat. where the men had left the van with the valet parking. At the time of the arrest the men were singing, Fill coffee carafe with water. Pour water into back of coffee maker. He: What to eat? I'd like a frigging bowl of cereal is what I'd like to eat. "You Don't Bring Me Flowers" accompanied on piano. Both were dressed in tuxedos and were heavily armed. Place carafe on burner of coffee maker. Turn on burner. She: You want cereal for dinner?

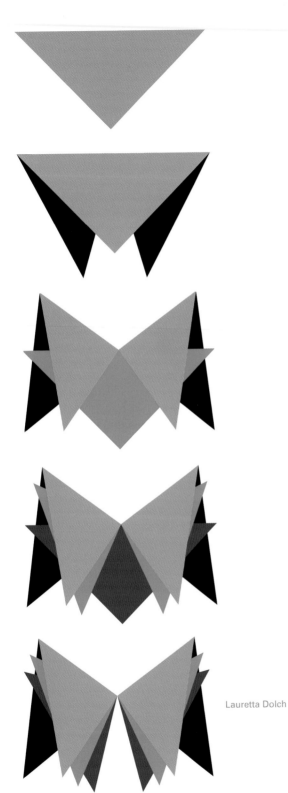

Physical, Virtual, and Temporal Layers In this project, designers began by creating a series of six-by-six-inch collages with four square sheets of colored paper. (We used origami paper). Each designer cut a square window into a larger sheet of paper so that they could move the colored sheets around and experiment with different designs.

In the second phase of the project, designers translated one of their physical collages into digital layers. Each physical layer became a separate layer in the digital file. They generated new compositions by digitally changing the color, scale, transparency, orientation, and position of the digital layers.

In the third phase, one digital composition became a style frame (the basis of a sequential animation). Each designer planned a sequence, approximately ten seconds long, that loops: that is, it begins and ends on an identical frame. They created nine-panel storyboards showing the sequence.

In the final phase, designers imported their style frames into a digital animation program (Flash), distributing each layer of the style frame to a layer in the timeline to create strata that change over time. Graphic Design II. Ellen Lupton, faculty.

Lauretta Dolch

Physical Layers

Digital Layers

Temporal Layers

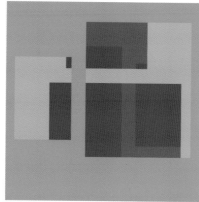

Windows Each layer is a window through which other layers are visible. Kelly Horigan.

Squares Complete, uncut squares move in and out of the frame. Doug Hucker.

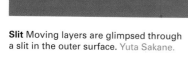
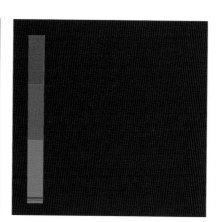

Slit Moving layers are glimpsed through a slit in the outer surface. Yuta Sakane.

Transparency

Transparency means a simultaneous perception of different spatial locations.... The position of the transparent figures has equivocal meaning as one sees each figure now as the closer, now as the farther one. Gyorgy Kepes

As a social value, transparency suggests clarity and directness. The idea of "transparent government" promotes processes that are open and understandable to the public, not hidden behind closed doors. Yet in design, transparency is often used not for the purposes of clarity, but to create dense, layered imagery built from veils of color and texture.

Any surface in the physical world is more or less transparent or opaque: a piece of wood has 100 percent opacity, while a room full of air has nearly zero. Image-editing software allows designers to adjust the opacity of any still or moving picture. Software lets you see through wood, or make air into a solid wall.

Transparency becomes an active design element when its value is somewhere between zero and 100 percent. In this chapter, we assume that a "transparent" image or surface is, generally, opaque to some degree. Indeed, you will discover that a surface built out of completely opaque elements can function in a transparent way.

Transparency and layers are related phenomena. A transparent square of color appears merely pale or faded until it passes over another shape or surface, allowing a second image to show through itself. A viewer thus perceives the transparency of one plane in relation to a second one. What is in front, and what is behind? What dominates, and what recedes?

Video and animation programs allow transparency to change over time. A fade is created by making a clip gradually become transparent. Dissolves occur when one clip fades out (becoming transparent) while a second clip fades in (becoming opaque).

This chapter begins by observing the properties of physical transparency, and then shows how to build transparent surfaces out of opaque graphic elements. We conclude by looking at the infinite malleability of digital transparency.

Transparency is a fascinating and seductive principle. How can it be used to build meaningful images? Transparency can serve to emphasize values of directness and clarity through adjustments and juxtapositions that maintain the wholeness or legibility of elements. Transparency also can serve to build complexity by allowing layers to mix and merge together. Transparency can be used thematically to combine or contrast ideas, linking levels of content. When used in a conscious and deliberate way, transparency contributes to the meaning and visual intrigue of a work of design.

Life History Historical and contemporary photographs and documents are layered over a satellite image from Google Earth of the land these people have inhabited. Transparency is used to separate the elements visually. Jeremy Botts, MFA Studio.

Water Jason Okutake

Physical Transparency

No material is wholly transparent. Ripples disturb the transparency of water, while air becomes thick with smoke or haze. Glass can be tinted, mirrored, cracked, etched, scratched, frosted, or painted to diminish its transparency. The reflective character of glass makes it partially opaque, an attribute that changes depending on light conditions.

A solid material such as wood or metal becomes transparent when its surface is perforated or interrupted. Venetian blinds shift from opaque to transparent as the slats slant open. Adjusting the blinds changes their degree of transparency.

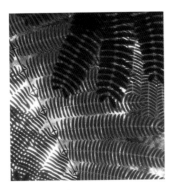

Tree Jeremy Botts

Veil Nancy Froehlich

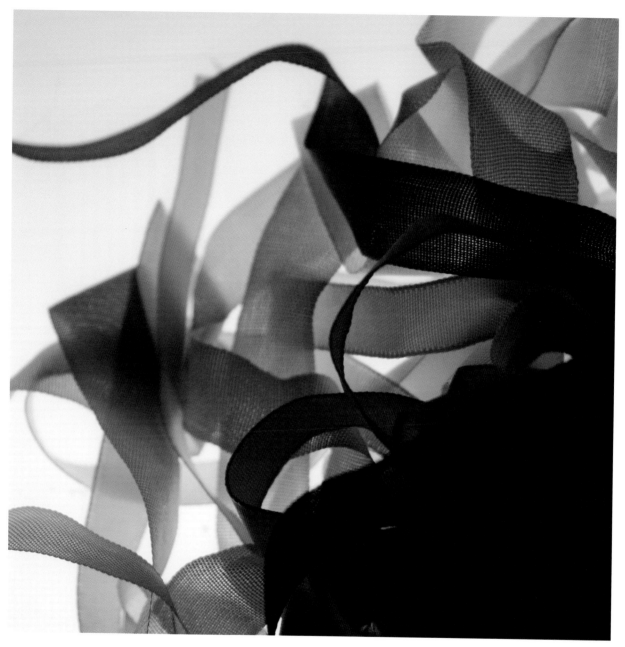

Ribbon Yue Tuo

Materials and Substances Observing
transparent objects and surfaces throughout
the physical environment yields countless
ideas for combining images and surfaces in
two-dimensional design. MFA Studio.

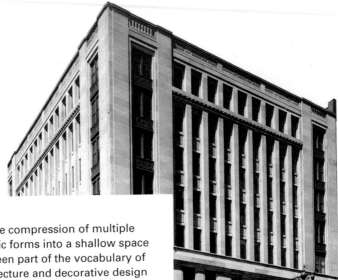

Graphic Transparency

Designers can translate the effects of physical transparency into overlapping layers of lines, shapes, textures, or letterforms. We call this phenomenon "graphic transparency." Just as in physical transparency, two or more surfaces are visible simultaneously, collapsed onto a single surface. A field of text placed over an image is transparent, revealing parts of the image through its open spaces.

The compression of multiple graphic forms into a shallow space has been part of the vocabulary of architecture and decorative design for hundreds of years. Traditional patterns such as plaid use colored thread to build up intersecting fields of color. Linear elements in classical and modern architecture, such as columns and moldings, often appear to pass through each other.[1]

Macmillan Company Building, New York, 1924. This early skyscraper employs vertical elements that span the upper stories of the building. The horizontal elements sit back behind the vertical surface, establishing a second plane that appears to pass continuously behind the front plane, like the threads in a plaid fabric. Architects: Carrère and Hastings with Shreve and Lamb. Vintage photograph.

1. On transparency in architecture, see Colin Rowe and Robert Slutzky, "Transparency: Literal and Phenomenal (Part 2)," in Joan Ockman, ed., *Architecture Culture, 1943–1968: A Documentary Anthology* (New York: Rizzoli, 1993), 205–25.

Plaid Fabric Traditional plaid fabrics are made by weaving together bands of colored thread over and under each other. Where contrasting colors mix, a new color appears. The horizontal and vertical stripes literally pass through each other on the same plane. Lee Jofa, *Carousel*, plaid fabric, cotton and rayon.

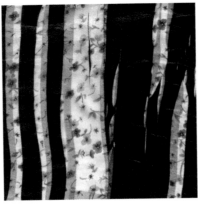

Over-Dyed Fabric To create this nontraditional print, fashion designer Han Feng bunched and folded a delicate floral print and then dyed it, creating long irregular stripes that sit on top of the floral pattern. The result is two competing planes of imagery compressed onto a single surface. Han Feng, polyester fabric.

If one sees two or more figures partly overlapping one another, and each of them claims for itself the common overlapped part, then one is confronted with a contradiction of spatial dimensions.

Typographic Plaid Layers of lines pass in front of a base text. The lines are like a slatted or perforated surface through which the text remains visible. Alissa Faden, MFA Studio.

Linear Transparency The letterforms in this pattern have been reduced to outlines, rendering them functionally transparent even as they overlap each other. Abbott Miller and Jeremy Hoffman, Pentagram, packaging for Mohawk Paper.

Graphic Transparency In each of these compositions, a photograph has been overlaid with a field of graphic elements. The graphic layer becomes an abstracted commentary on the image underneath. MFA Studio.

Jeremy Botts

Jason Okutake

100 percent opacity

50 percent opacity. Fade-to-black is a standard transition in film and video.

Digital Transparency

Imaging software allows designers to alter the opacity of nearly any graphic element, including type, photographs, and moving images. To do this, the software employs an algorithm that multiplies the tonal values of one layer against those of another, generating a mix between the two layers. To make any image transparent involves compromising its intensity, lowering its overall contrast.

Transparency is used not only to mix two visual elements, but also to make one image fade out against its background. In video and animation, such fades occur over time. The most common technique is the fade-to-black, which employs the default black background. The resulting clip gradually loses intensity while becoming darker. Video editors create a fade-to-white by placing a white background behind the clip. The same effects are used in print graphics to change the relationship between an image and its background.

Transparent type, opaque image

Transparency in type and image

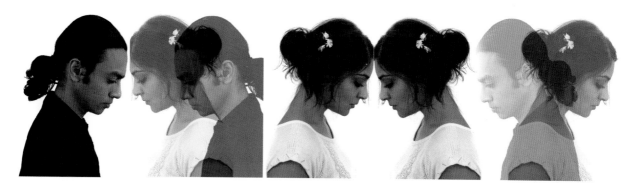

Opposites Attract Transparency serves
to build relationships between images.
Here, male and female mix and overlap.
Jason Okutake, MFA Studio.

Life Lines Transparent layers of text and image
intersect. Kelley McIntyre, MFA Studio.

Wall Flowers Transparent layers build
up to make a dense frame or cartouche.
Jeremy Botts, MFA Studio.

Seeing Through This composition builds relationships between layers of graphic elements and an underlying photograph. The designer has manipulated the elements graphically as well as changing their digital transparency. Yue Tuo, MFA Studio. Photography: Nancy Froehlich.

Modularity

Two eight-stud LEGO bricks can be combined in twenty-four ways.
Three eight-stud LEGO bricks can be combined in 1,060 ways.
Six eight-stud LEGO bricks can be combined in 102,981,500 ways.
With eight bricks the possibilities are virtually endless.

The Ultimate LEGO Book

Every design problem is completed within a set of constraints or limitations. These limits can be as broad as "design a logo," as generic as "print on standard letter paper," or as narrow as "arrange six circles in a square space." Working within the constraints of a problem is part of the fun and challenge of design.

Modularity is a special kind of constraint. A module is a fixed element used within a larger system or structure. For example, a pixel is a module that builds a digital image. A pixel is so small, we rarely stop to notice it, but when designers create pixel-based typefaces, they use a grid of pixels to invent letterforms that are consistent from one to the next while giving each one a distinctive shape.

A nine-by-nine grid of pixels can yield an infinite number of different typefaces. Likewise, a tiny handful of LEGO bricks contains an astonishing number of possible combinations.[1] The endless variety of forms occurs, however, within the strict parameters of the system, which permits just one basic kind of connection.

Building materials—from bricks to lumber to plumbing parts— are manufactured in standard sizes. By working with ready-made materials, an architect helps control construction costs while also streamlining the design process.

Designers are constantly making decisions about size, color, placement, proportion, relationships, and materials as well as about subject matter, style, and imagery. Sometimes, the decision-making process can be so overwhelming, it's hard to know how to begin and when to stop. When a few factors are determined in advance, the designer is free to think about other parts of the problem. A well-defined constraint can free up the thought process by taking some decisions off the table. In creating a page of typography, for example, a designer can choose to work within the constraints of one or two type families, and then explore different combinations of size, weight, and placement within that family of elements.

The book you are reading is organized around a typographic grid whose basic module is a square. By accepting the square unit as a given, we were able to mix and match images while creating a feeling of continuity across the book. The square units vary in size, however (keeping the layouts from getting dull), and some pictures stretch across more than one module (or ignore the grid altogether). Rules are helpful, but it's fun to break them.

Post-it Wallpaper This wall installation was built solely from three colors of Post-it neon note sheets, creating the optical effect of an enlarged halftone image or modular supergraphic. Nolen Strals and Bruce Willen, Post Typography.

1. *The Ultimate LEGO Book* (New York: DK Publishing, 1999).

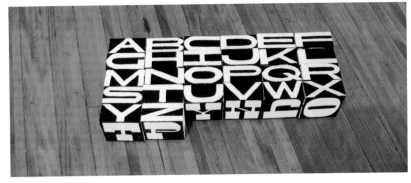

Alphabet Blocks These rectangular wooden blocks have a different alphabet painted on each side. Nolen Strals and Bruce Willen, Post Typography.

Working with Constraints

In the projects shown here, graphic designers have used modular elements to produce unpredictable results. Try looking at familiar systems from a fresh angle. Given the constraints of any system, how can you play with the rules to make something new?

A child's set of alphabet blocks looks a certain way, for example, because the blocks are made from perfect cubes. But what if alphabet blocks were made from rectangles instead of cubes? The oddly proportioned faces of the blocks at left provided a framework for designing new letterforms in response to the constraints provided by the blocks of wood.

Standard materials such as laser paper are often used in generic ways. A standard sheet of office paper can be very dull indeed. Yet with creative thinking, an ordinary piece of paper can be used for dramatic effect. The temporary signage program shown on the opposite page employs economical processes and everyday materials to produce graphics at a lavish scale—at a very low cost.

Stedlijk Museum CS Signage System This sign system was created for the temporary headquarters of a major museum in the Netherlands. The basic module is a plastic document holder, into which standard sheets of A4 letter paper are inserted. Large-scale graphics are tiled across multiple plastic envelopes. Experimental Jetset.

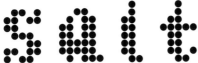

Colin Ford

Clean and Dirty Systems Working with a nine-by-nine-square grid of circles, students created four letterforms with common characteristics such as weight, proportion, and density.

After creating a consistent and well-structured set of characters, the students introduced decay, degradation, distortion, randomness, or physicality into the design. The underlying structure becomes an armature for new and unexpected processes.

Approaches to making the clean system dirty include graphic techniques such as applying a filter to the source image or systematically varying the elements, as well as using physical techniques such as painting, stitching, or assembling. Typography I. Ellen Lupton, faculty.

Kristen Bennett

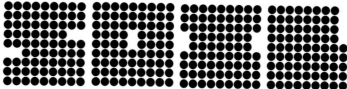

Emily Goldfarb

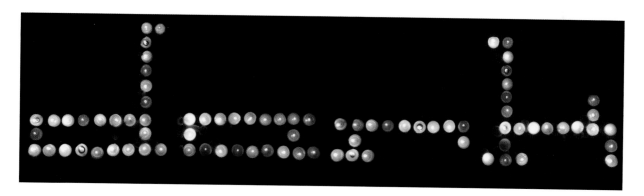

Nicolette Cornelius

Austin Roesberg

Andy Bonner

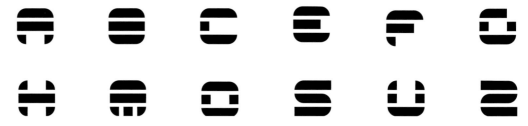

Zachary Richter

Modular Alphabet In these examples, designers created systems of characters using three basic shapes: a square (each side equals one unit), a rectangle (one unit by two units), and a quarter-circle (radius equals one unit). Shapes could be assembled in any way, but their relative scale could not change.

Some forms are dense and solid, while others are split apart. Some use the curved elements to shape the outer edge, while others use curves to cut away the interior. Most have a simple profile, but it is also possible to build a detailed texture out of smaller-scaled elements. Experimental Typography. Nolen Strals and Bruce Willen, faculty.

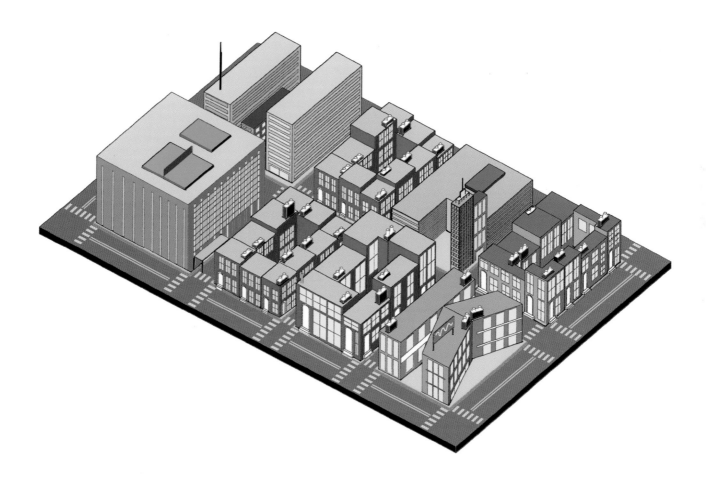

Architectural Alphabet The three-dimensional
design software AutoCAD has been used to
spell out the phrase "word book" in buildings.
The rectilinear modules of architecture
become the building blocks for letterforms.
Johanna Barthmaier, Typography I. Ellen
Lupton, faculty.

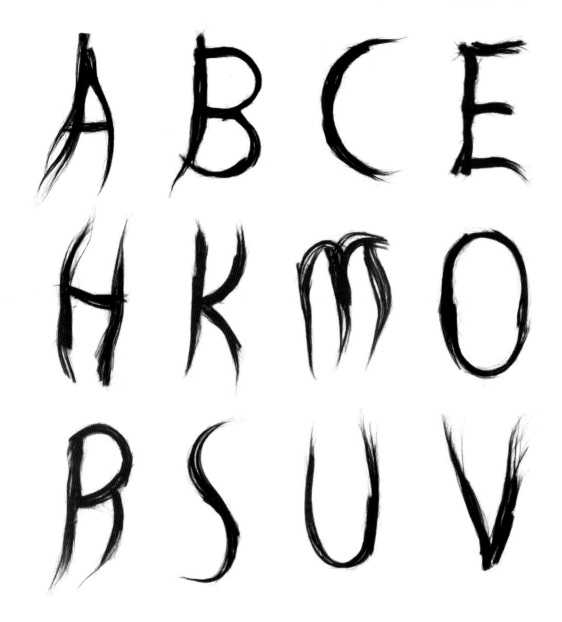

Ready-made Alphabet The challenge here was to create a set of characters using objects from the environment rather than drawing them digitally or by hand. The designers discovered letterforms hidden in the things around them. Experimental Typography. Nolen Strals and Bruce Willen, faculty.

Jennifer Baghieri

Oliver Munday

Symbol Systems

A symbol stands for or represents objects, functions, and processes. Many familiar symbols, such as McDonald's golden arches, are highly distilled, stripped of extraneous detail, delivering just enough information to convey meaning. Symbol systems are often based on geometric modules that come together to create myriad forms and functions.

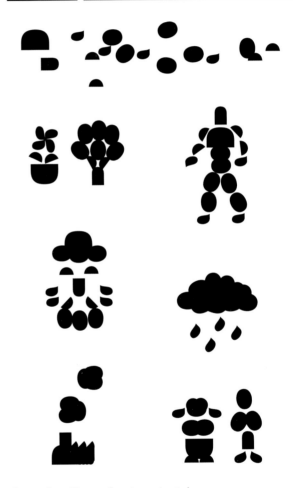

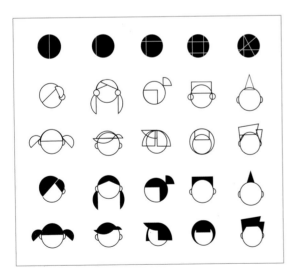

Modular Hairdos Geometrically derived forms combine to shape myriad hair styles. Yue Tuo, MFA Studio.

Counterform Pictures Counters extracted from letters in a title cohere into visual narratives. Nolen Strals and Bruce Willen, Post Typography.

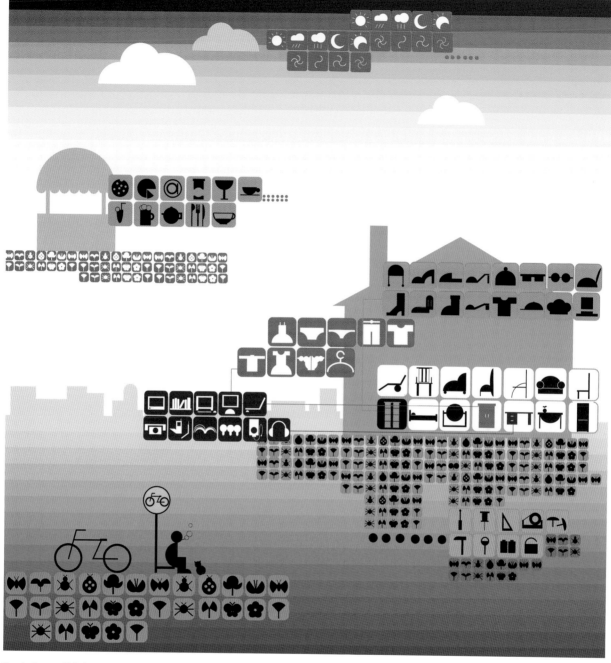

Symbolscape This landscape is built and described by a series of modularly structured symbols stacked and layered to denote fauna, flora, and form. Yue Tuo, MFA Studio.

Pixel Art The image above is built from a modular grid of squares, colored and combined to make a highly pixilated social scene. Pixels are the building block of any digital image. Here, they become an expressive element. April Osmanof, MFA Studio.

Pixel Effects Like a Chuck Close painting,
this photographic detail takes on an abstract
quality when enlarged—smooth, graduated,
tonal hues divide into elemental square
segments. April Osmanof, MFA Studio.
Photograph: Marc Alain.

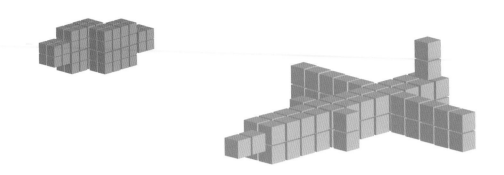

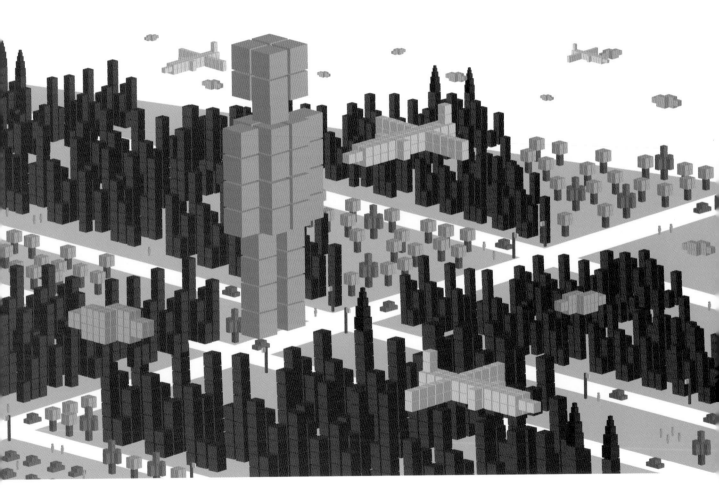

A City of Cubes An urban landscape teems with people, planes, clouds, automobiles, skyscrapers, and trees—all built from cubes in Adobe Illustrator. Yong Seuk Lee, MFA Studio.

Extrapolations in Excel These elaborate drawings utilize the gridded compartments of an Excel spreadsheet as a catalyst and a constraint. Danielle Aubert, MFA thesis, Yale University School of Art.

Grid

Typography is mostly an act of **dividing** a limited surface. Willi Baumeister

A grid is a network of lines. The lines in a grid typically run horizontally and vertically in evenly paced increments, but grids can be angled, irregular, or even circular as well.

When you write notes on a pad of lined paper, or sketch out a floor plan on graph paper, or practice handwriting or calligraphy on ruled pages, the lines serve to guide the hand and eye as you work.

Grids function similarly in the design of printed matter. Guidelines help the designer align elements in relation to each other. Consistent margins and columns create an underlying structure that unifies the pages of a document and makes the layout process more efficient. In addition to organizing the active content of the page (text and images), the grid lends structure to the white spaces, which cease to be merely blank and passive voids but participate in the rhythm of the overall system.

A well-made grid encourages the designer to vary the scale and placement of elements without relying wholly on arbitrary or whimsical judgments. The grid offers a rationale and a starting point for each composition, converting a blank area into a structured field.

Flag Wall Grids appear throughout the built environment, revealing both order and decay. Jason Okutake, MFA Studio.

Many artists have embraced the grid as a rational, universal form that exists outside of the individual producer. At the same time, the grid is culturally associated with modern urbanism, architecture, and technology. The facades of many glass high rises and other modern buildings consist of uniform ribbons of metal and glass that wrap the building's volume in a continuous skin. In contrast with the symmetrical hierarchy of a classical building, with its strong entranceway and tiered pattern of windows, a gridded facade expresses a democracy of elements.

Grids function throughout society. The street grids used in many modern cities around the globe promote circulation among neighborhoods and the flow of traffic, in contrast with the suburban cul de sac, a dead-end road that keeps neighborhoods closed off and private.

The grid imparts a similarly democratic character to the printed page. By marking space into numerous equal units, the grid makes the entire page available for use; the edges become as important as the center. Grids help designers create active, asymmetrical compositions in place of static, centered ones. By breaking down space into smaller units, grids encourage designers to leave some areas open rather than filling up the whole page.

Software interfaces encourage the use of grids by making it easy to establish margins, columns, and page templates. Guidelines can be quickly dragged, dropped, and deleted and made visible or invisible at will. (Indeed, it is a good idea when working on screen to switch off the guidelines from time to time, as they can create a false sense of fullness and structure as well as clutter one's view.)

This chapter looks at the grid as a means of generating form, arranging images, and organizing information. The grid can work quietly in the background, or it can assert itself as an active element. The grid becomes visible as objects come into alignment with it. Some designers use grids in a strict, absolute way, while others see them as a starting point in an evolving process. This book is designed with a strong grid, but when an image or layout needs to break step with the regiment, it is allowed to do so.

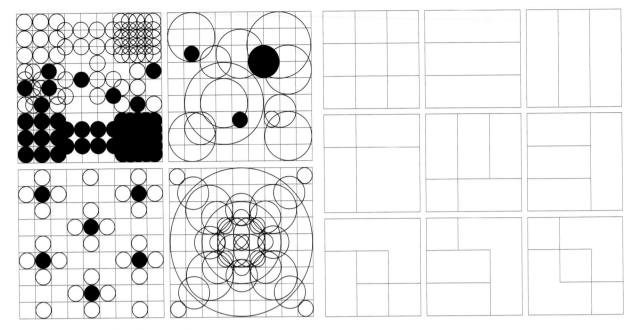

Grids Generate Form The cells and nodes of a grid can be used to generate complex pattern designs as well as simple rectangles. Dividing a square into nine identical units is a classic design problem. Numerous simple forms and relationships can be built against this simple matrix. Jason Okutake and John P. Corrigan, MFA Studio.

Form and Content

The grid has a long history within modern art and design as a means for generating form. You can construct compositions, layouts, and patterns by dividing a space into fields and filling in or delineating its cells in different ways. Try building irregular and asymmetric compositions against the neutral, ready-made backdrop of a grid. The same formal principles apply to organizing text and images in a publication design.

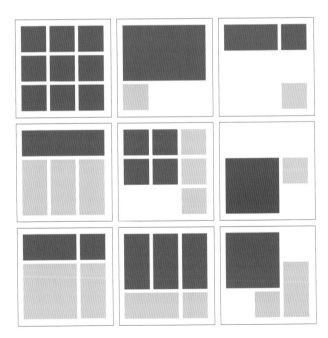

Grids Organize Content The nine-square grid divides the page into spaces for images and text. Although each layout has its own rhythm and scale, the pages are unified by the grid's underlying structure. The book you are reading is built around a similar nine-square grid. John P. Corrigan, MFA Studio.

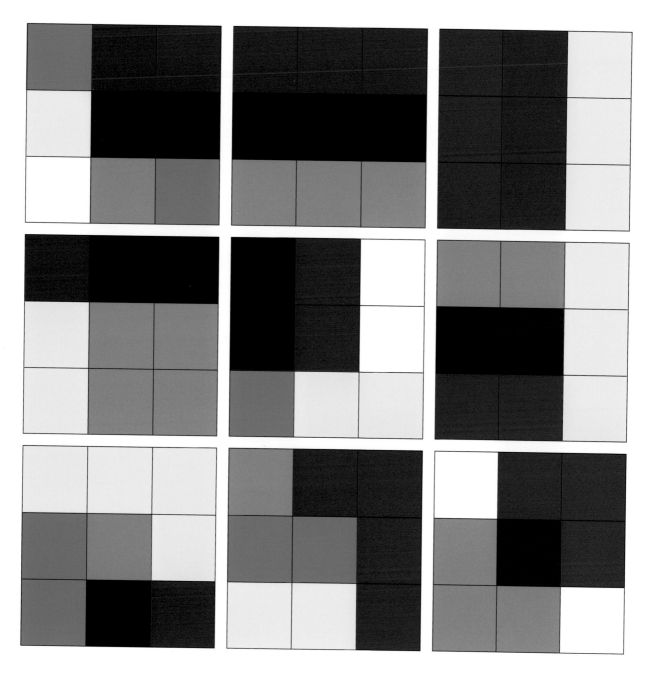

Nine-square Grid: Color Fields The grid
provides a structure for organizing fields
of color that frame and overlap each other.
Complexity emerges against a simple
armature. John P. Corrigan, MFA Studio.

Strict Grid Here, the rigidly imposed grid emphasizes the flat, graphic character and head-on viewpoint of the photographs. Jeremy Botts, MFA Studio.

Broken Grid The rectilinear photographs
overlap and misalign to create a sense of
movement and depth. Individually, each image
is static, but together, they convey action
and change. John P. Corrigan, MFA Studio.

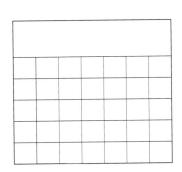

Monthly Calendar The column and row structure of the familiar monthly calendar is open to reinterpretation. Graphic Design I. Kim Bost, faculty.

Calendar Grid

Standard calendar designs use columns and rows to organize the weeks and days that make up a month. The days of the week align in vertical columns, while each week occupies a horizontal row. This form has become standard and universal, as have various templates used in day planners.

Developing alternate ways to structure a calendar is a good design challenge. The underlying problem in any calendar design is to use two-dimensional space to represent a sequence in time. The grid can be circular, diagonal, or freeform.

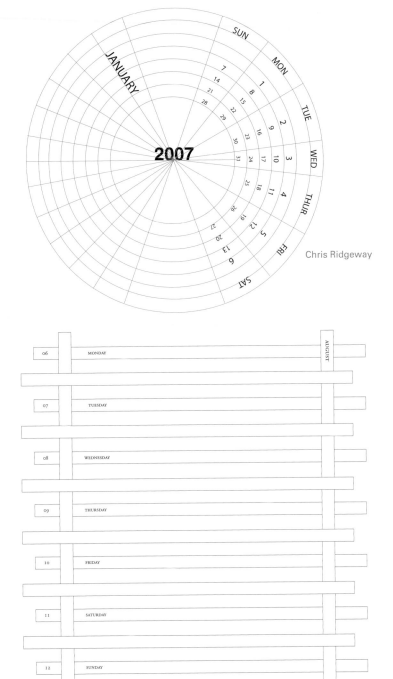

Chris Ridgeway

Jessica Neil

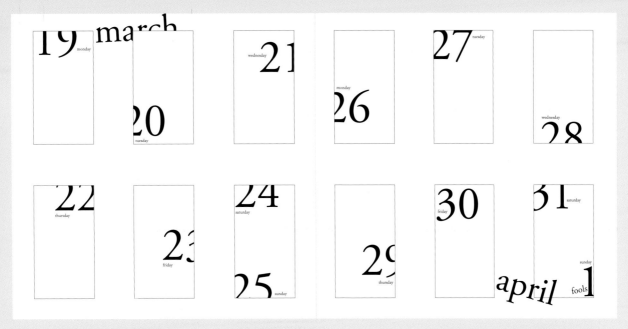

19 monday march
20 tuesday
wednesday 21
22 thursday
23 friday
24 saturday
25 sunday
26 monday
27 tuesday
wednesday 28
29 thursday
30 friday
31 saturday
april fools 1 sunday

April Osmanof

MON	AUGUST TWENTIETH	AUGUST TWENTY SEVENTH	MON
TUE	AUGUST TWENTY FIRST	AUGUST TWENTY EIGHTH	TUE
WED	AUGUST TWENTY SECOND	AUGUST TWENTY NINTH	WED
THR	AUGUST TWENTY THIRD	AUGUST THIRTIETH	THR
FRI	AUGUST TWENTY FOURTH	AUGUST THIRTY FIRST	FRI
SAT	AUGUST TWENTY FIFTH	SEPTEMBER FIRST	SAT
SUN	AUGUST TWENTY SIXTH	SEPTEMBER SECOND	SUN

Lindsey Sherman

Weekly Calendar These pages and spreads from a day planner organize the days of the week and provide space for users to record notes. Typography I. Ellen Lupton, faculty.

One column

Two columns

Three columns

Four columns

Page Grids

A standard textbook is designed with a one-column grid: a single block of body copy is surrounded by margins that function as a simple frame for the content. For hundreds of years, Bibles have been designed with pages divided into two columns. Textbooks, dictionaries, reference manuals, and other books containing large amounts of text often use a two-column grid, breaking up space and making the pages less overwhelming for readers.

Magazines typically use grids with three or more vertical divisions. Multiple columns guide the placement of text, headlines, captions, images, and other page elements. One or more horizontal "hang lines" provide additional structure. A skilled designer uses a grid actively, not passively, allowing the modules to suggest intriguing shapes and surprising placements for elements.

Multicolumn Grid This complex design is built around a four-column grid structure. It comments on medieval book design traditions. Charles Calixto, Typography I. Ellen Lupton, faculty.

Many Columns, Many Choices The page layouts shown here from *Print* magazine, designed by Pentagram, employ a complex, multicolumn grid. The column structure gives the pages their vertical grain, while horizontal hang lines anchor each spread, bringing elements into taut alignment. The grid helps the layout designer create active, varied pages that are held together by an underlying structure. The grid accommodates a mix of sizes and proportions in both image and text blocks. And, where appropriate, the designer breaks the grid altogether. Abbott Miller and John Kudos, Pentagram. *Print* magazine.

Pattern

The **principles** discoverable in the works
of the past belong to us; not so the **results**.

Owen Jones

The creative evolution of ornament spans all of human history. Shared ways to generate pattern are found in cultures around the world. Universal principles underlie diverse styles and icons that speak to particular times and traditions.

This chapter shows how to build complex patterns around core concepts. Dots, stripes, and grids provide the architecture behind an infinite range of designs. By composing a single element in different schemes, the designer can create endless variations, building complexity around a logical core.

Styles and motifs of pattern-making evolve within and among cultures, and they move in and out of fashion. They travel from place to place and time to time, carried along like viruses by the forces of commerce and the restless desire for variety.

In the twentieth century, modern designers avoided ornate detail in favor of minimal adornment. In 1908, the Viennese design critic Adolf Loos famously conflated "Ornament and Crime." He linked the human lust for decoration with primitive tattoos and criminal behavior.[1]

Yet despite the modern distaste for ornament, the structural analysis of pattern is central to modern design theory. In 1856, Owen Jones created his monumental *Grammar of Ornament*, documenting decorative vocabularies from around the world.[2] Jones's book encouraged Western designers to copy and reinterpret "exotic" motifs from Asia and Africa, but it also helped them recognize principles that unite an endless diversity of forms.

Today, surface pattern is creating a vibrant discourse. The rebirth of ornament is linked to the revival of craft in architecture, products, and interiors, as well as to scientific views of how life emerges from the interaction of simple rules.

The decorative forms presented in this chapter embrace a mix of formal structure and organic irregularity. They meld individual authorship with rule-based systems, and they merge formal abstraction with personal narrative. By understanding how to produce patterns, designers learn how to weave complexity out of elementary structures, participating in the world's most ancient and prevalent artistic practice.

Crazy Quilt Mixing and matching patterns is an ancient enterprise. Here, a mix is made with a palette of digital elements that communicate with each other. Jeremy Botts, MFA Studio.

1. Adolf Loos, *Ornament and Crime: Selected Essays* (Riverside, CA: Ariadne Press, 1998).
2. Owen Jones, *The Grammar of Ornament* (London: Day and Son, 1856).

The secret to success in all ornament is the production of a broad general effect by the repetition of **a few simple elements**.

Owen Jones

Dots, Stripes, and Grids

In the nineteenth century, designers began analyzing how patterns are made. They found that nearly any pattern arises from three basic forms: isolated elements, linear elements, and the criss-crossing or interaction of the two.[1] Various terms have been used to name these elementary conditions, but we will call them dots, stripes, and grids.

Any isolated form can be considered a dot, from a simple circle to an ornate flower. A stripe, in contrast, is a linear path. It can consist of a straight, solid line, or it can be built up from smaller elements (dots) that link together visually to form a line.

These two basic structures, dots and stripes, interact to form grids. As a grid takes shape, it subverts the identity of the separate elements in favor of a larger texture. Indeed, creating that larger texture is what pattern design is all about. Imagine a field of wildflowers. It is filled with spectacular individual organisms that contribute to an overall system.

1. Our scheme for classifying ornament is adapted from Archibald Christie, *Traditional Methods of Pattern Designing; An Introduction to the Study of the Decorative Art* (Oxford: Clarendon Press, 1910).

From Point to Line to Grid As dots move together, they form into lines and other shapes (while still being dots). As stripes cross over each other and become grids, they cut up the field into new figures, which function like new dots or new stripes.

Some of the most visually fascinating patterns result from figure/ground ambiguity. The identity of a form can oscillate between being a figure (dot, stripe) to being a ground or support for another, opposing figure.

Repeating Elements

How does a simple form—a dot, a square, a flower, a cross—populate a surface to create a pattern that calms, pleases, or surprises us?

Whether rendered by hand, machine, or code, a pattern results from repetition. An army of dots can be regulated by a rigid geometric grid, or it can randomly swarm across a surface via irregular handmade marks. It can spread out in a continuous veil or concentrate its forces in pockets of intensity.

In every instance, however, patterns follow some repetitive principle, whether dictated by a mechanical grid, a digital algorithm, or the physical rhythm of a craftsperson's tool as it works along a surface.

In the series of pattern studies developed here and on the following pages, a simple lozenge form is used to build designs of varying complexity. Experiments of this kind can be performed with countless base shapes, yielding an endless range of individual results.

One Element, Many Patterns The basic element in these patterns is a lozenge shape. Based on the orientation, proximity, scale, and color of the lozenges, they group into overlapping lines, forming a nascent grid. Jeremy Botts, MFA Studio.

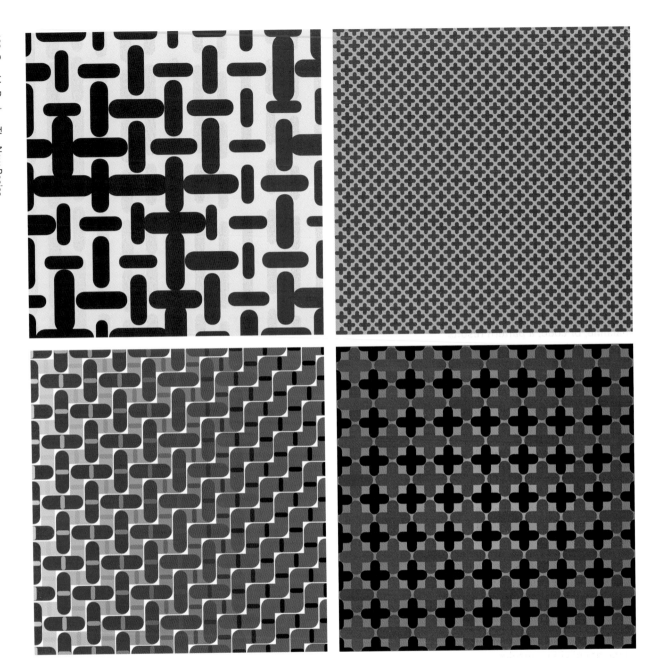

One Element, Many Patterns In this series of designs, the lozenge shape functions as a dot, the primitive element at the core of numerous variations. This oblong dot combines with other dots to form quatrefoils (a new super-dot) as well as lines.

As lozenges of common color or orientation begin to associate with each other visually, additional figures take shape across the surface. Jeremy Botts, MFA Studio.

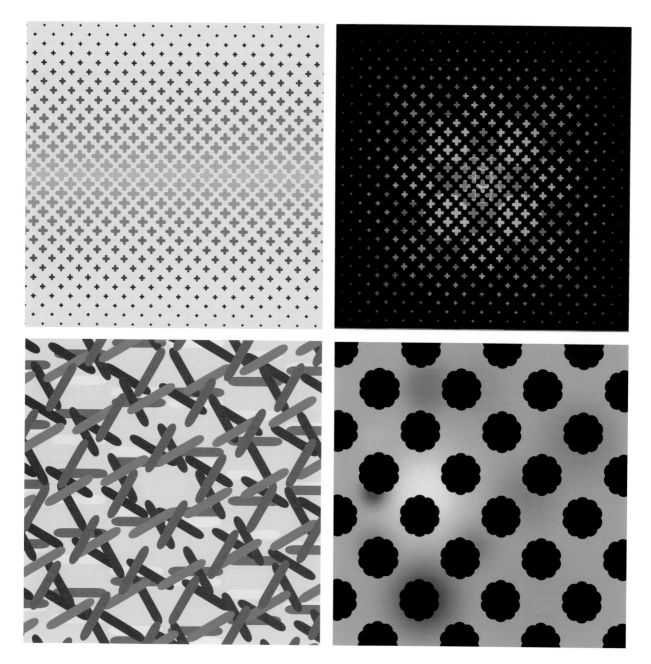

Changing Color, Scale, and Orientation
Altering the color contrast between elements or changing the overall scale of the pattern transforms its visual impact. Color shifts can be uniform across the surface, or they can take place in gradients or steps.

Turning elements on an angle or changing their scale also creates a sense of depth and motion. New figures emerge as the lonzenge rotates and repeats. Jeremy Botts, MFA Studio.

Iconic Patterns Here, traditional pattern structures have been populated with images that have personal significance for the designer: popsicles, bombs, bungee cords, yellow camouflage, and slices of bright green cake. The single tiles above can be repeated into larger patterns, as shown opposite. Spence Holman, MFA Studio.

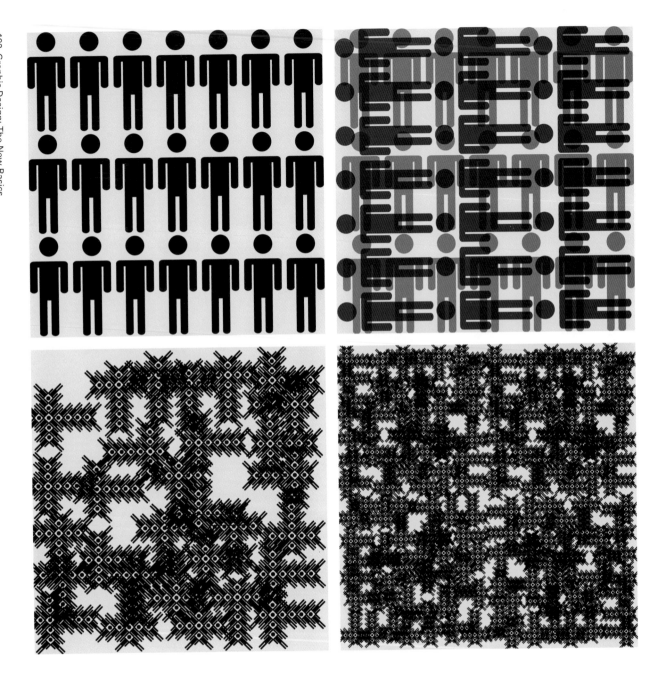

Regular and Irregular Interesting pattern designs often result from a mix of regular and irregular forces as well as abstract and recognizable imagery. Here, regimented rows of icons overlap to create dense crowds as well as orderly battalions. Yong Seuk Lee, MFA Studio.

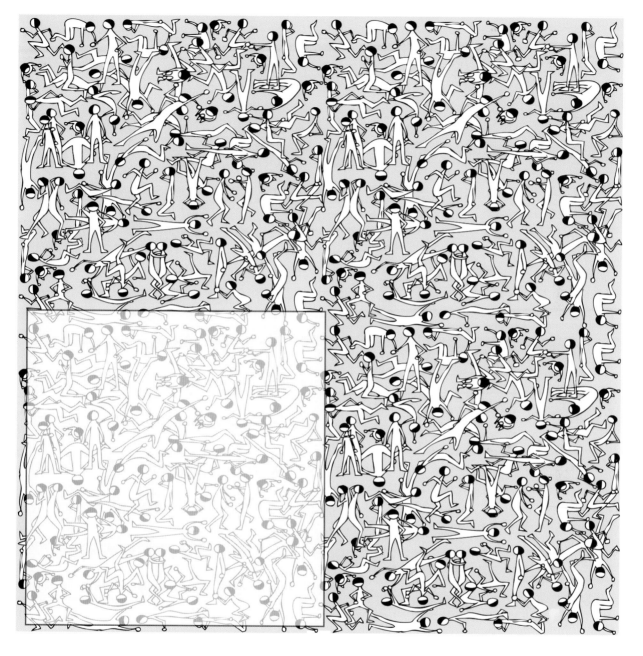

Random Repeat These patterns appear highly irregular, yet they are composed of repeating tiles. To make this kind of pattern, the designer needs to make the left and right edges and the top and bottom edges match up with those of an identical tile. Anything can take place in the middle of the tile.

The tiles shown here are square, but they could be rectangles, diamonds, or any other interlocking shape. Yong Seuk Lee, MFA Studio.

Grid as Matrix An infinite number of patterns can be created from a common grid. In the simplest patterns, each cell is turned on or off. Larger figures take shape as neighboring clusters fill in.

More complex patterns occur when the grid serves to locate forms without dictating their outlines or borders. Jason Okutake, MFA Studio.

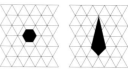

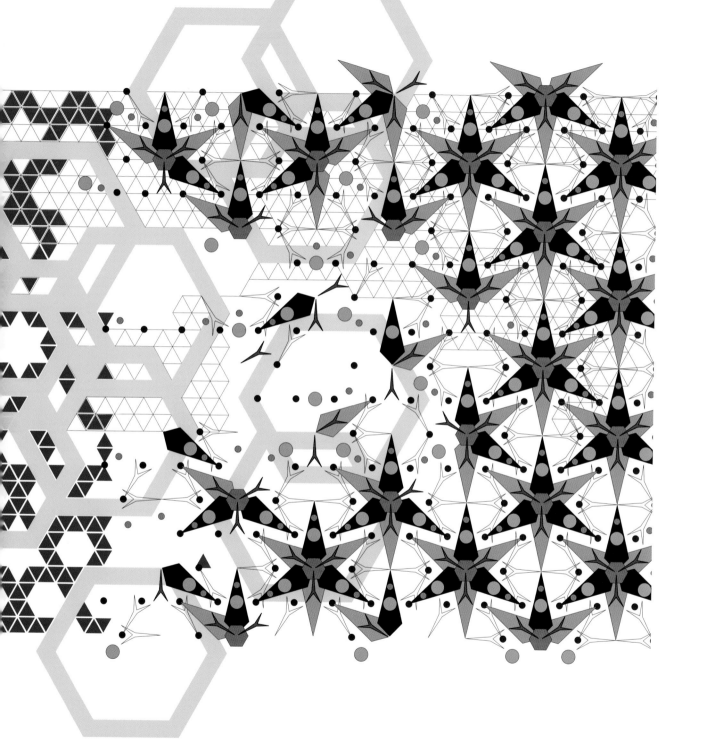

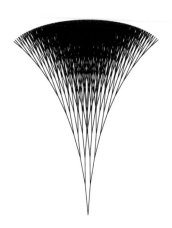

Code-Based Patterns

Every pattern follows a rule. Defining rules with computer code allows the designer to create variations by changing the input to the system. The designer creates the rule, but the end result may be unexpected.

The patterns shown here were designed using Processing, the open-source computer language created for designers and visual artists. All the patterns are built around the basic form of a binary tree, a structure in which every node yields no more than two offspring. New branches appear with each iteration of the program.

The binary tree form has been repeated, rotated, inverted, connected, and overlapped to generate a variety of pattern elements, equivalent to "tiles" in a traditional design. By varying the inputs to the code, the designer created four different tiles, which she joined together in Photoshop to produce a larger repeating pattern. The principle is no different from that used in many traditional ornamental designs, but the process has been automated, yielding a different kind of density.

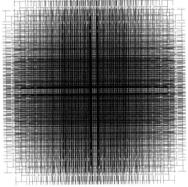

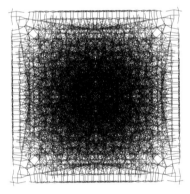

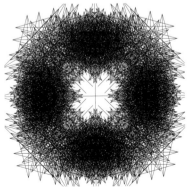

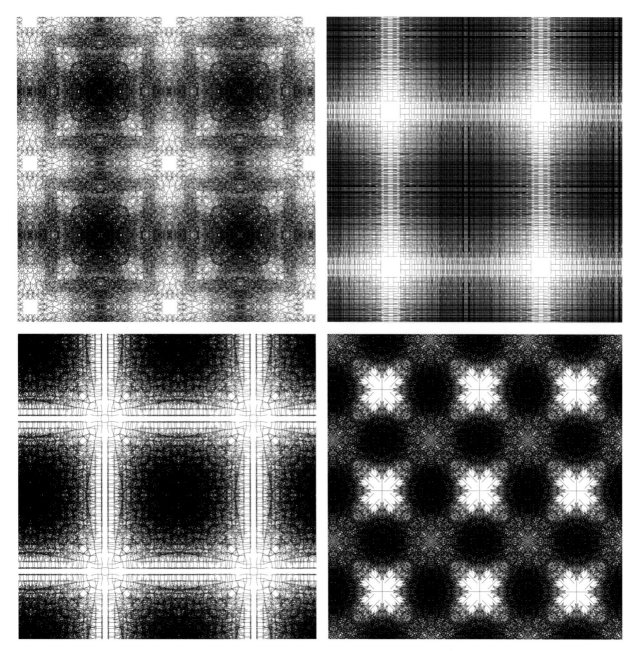

Vary the Input Four different base elements
were created by varying the input to the
code. The base "tiles" are joined together
to create a repeat pattern; new figures
emerge where the tiles come together,
just as in traditional ornament. Yeohyun Ahn,
Interactive Media II. James Ravel, faculty.

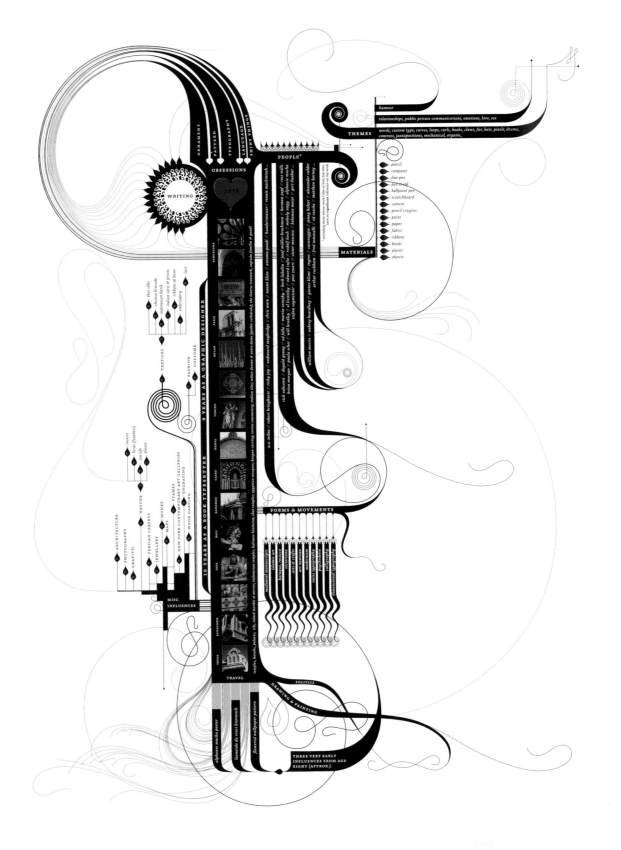

Diagram

In emphasizing evidential quality and beauty, I also want to move the practices of **analytical design** far away from the practices of propaganda, marketing, graphic design, and commercial art.

Edward R. Tufte

A diagram is a graphic representation of a structure, situation, or process. Diagrams can depict the anatomy of a creature, the hierarchy of a corporation, or the flow of ideas. Diagrams allow us to see relationships that would not come forward in a straight list of numbers or a verbal description.

Many of the visual elements and phenomena described in this book—from point, line, and plane to scale, color, hierarchy, layers, and more—converge in the design of diagrams. In the realm of information graphics, the aesthetic role of these elements remains important, but something else occurs as well. Graphic marks and visual relationships take on specific meanings, coded within the diagram to depict numerical increments, relative size, temporal change, structural links, and other conditions.

The great theorist of information design is Edward R. Tufte, who has been publishing books on this subject since 1983. Tufte finds a certain kind of beauty in the visual display of data—a universal beauty grounded in the laws of nature and the mind's ability to comprehend them.[1]

Tufte has called for removing the practice of information design from the distorting grasp of propaganda and graphic design. He argues that a chart or diagram should employ no metaphoric distractions or excessive flourishes (what he has called "chart junk"), but should stay within the realm of objective observation.

Tufte's purist point of view is profound and compelling, but it may be overly restrictive. Information graphics do have a role to play in the realm of expressive and editorial graphics. The language of diagrams has yielded a rich and evocative repertoire within contemporary design. In editorial contexts, diagrams often function to illuminate and explain complex ideas. They can be clean and reductive or richly expressive, creating evocative pictures that reveal surprising relationships and impress the eye with the sublime density and grandeur of a body of data.

Many of the examples developed in this chapter are rigorous but not pure. Some pieces use diagrams to depict personal histories, a process that forces the designer to develop systematic ways to represent subjective experience. Such an approach is seen in the extravagant autobiographical diagram presented on the page opposite, by Marian Bantjes. Her map does not aim to convey evidence in a strictly scientific way, but rather uses analytical thinking to unleash a language that is both personal and universal, building complexity around basic structures.

1. Edward R. Tufte, *Beautiful Evidence* (Cheshire, CT: Graphics Press, 2006).

Map of Influences This alluring diagram by designer and artist Marian Bantjes describes her visual influences, which range from medieval and Celtic lettering, to baroque and rococo ornament, to Swiss typography and American psychedelia. Those diverse influences come alive in the flowing, filigreed lines of the piece. Marian Bantjes.

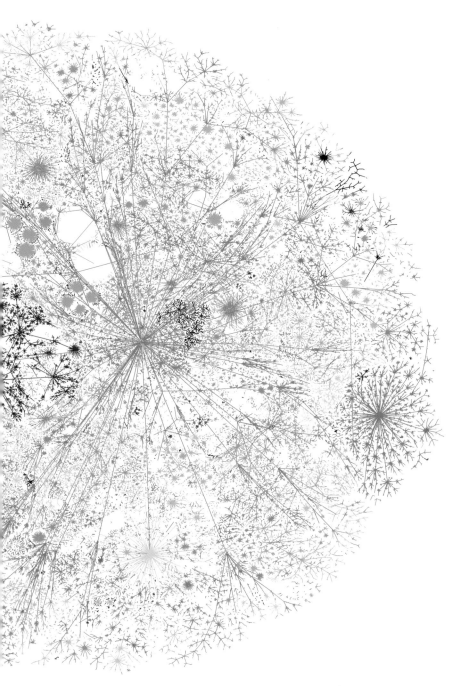

Making Connections
A network, also called a graph, is a set of connections among nodes or points.[1] There are various ways to connect the nodes in a network, resulting in different kinds of organization. Centralized networks include pyramids and trees, where all power issues from a common point. A decentralized network has a spine with radiating elements, as in an interstate highway system. A distributed network has node-to-node relationships with no spine and no center. The Internet is a distributed network peppered with concentrated nodes of connectivity.

Networks are everywhere—not just in technology, but throughout nature and society. A food chain, a city plan, and the pathway of a disease are all networks that can be described graphically with points and lines.

Decentralized Network This snapshot of the World Wide Web (detail) shows the connections among servers. A relatively small number of hubs dominate global traffic. Courtesy Lumeta Corp. © 2005 Lumeta Corp.

1. On network theory, see Alexander Galloway and Eugene Thacker, "Protocol, Control and Networks," *Grey Room* 12 (Fall 2004): 6–29. See also Christopher Alexander, "The City is Not a Tree," in Joan Ockman, ed., *Architecture Culture, 1943–1968: A Documentary Anthology* (New York: Rizzoli, 1993), 379–88.

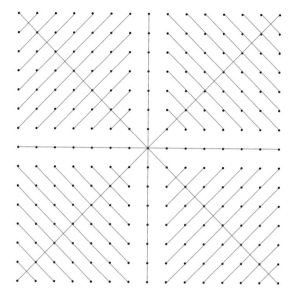

Centralized Kelly Horigan

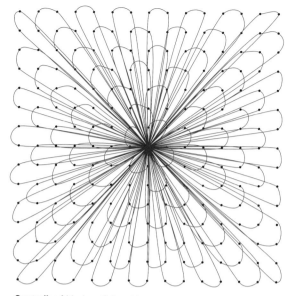

Centralized Lindsay Orlowski

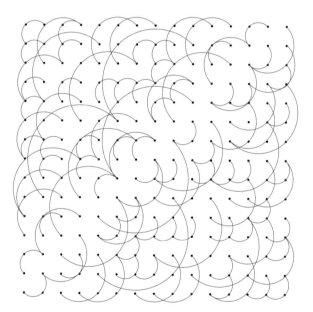

Decentralized Lindsay Orlowski

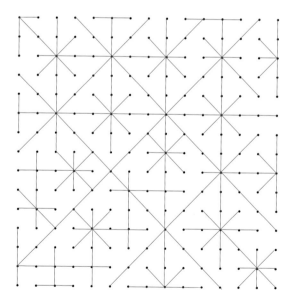

Distributed Kelly Horigan

Designing Networks In this project, designers connect a grid of dots with lines, producing designs that reflect different types of networks: centralized, decentralized, and distributed. Graphic Design II. Ellen Lupton, faculty.

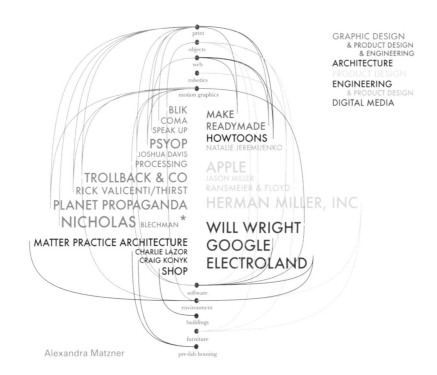

GRAPHIC DESIGN
& PRODUCT DESIGN
& ENGINEERING
ARCHITECTURE
PRODUCT DESIGN
ENGINEERING
& PRODUCT DESIGN
DIGITAL MEDIA

Alexandra Matzner

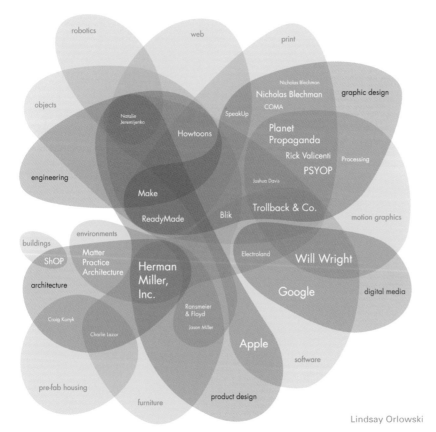

Lindsay Orlowski

Overlapping Relationships People don't fall into tidy categories. Any individual can have many identities: parent, child, professional, fan, taxpayer, and so on.

In the project shown here, students were given a list of designers and design firms who work in different fields (graphic design, architecture, and new media) and who produce different kinds of projects (buildings, websites, products, print, and so on). The list also ranked people according to the size of their firms (from single practitioners to large corporations). The design challenge was to represent these overlapping categories visually, using typography, scale, color, line, and other cues to indicate connections and differences.

Some of the solutions use dots of varying size to indicate scale or to mark points on a conceptual map. Others change the size of the typography to indicate the scale. Overlapping planes or crossing lines were used to indicate areas of overlap. This problem can be applied to any collection of objects, from a grocery list to categories of music or art. Graphic Design II. Ellen Lupton, faculty.

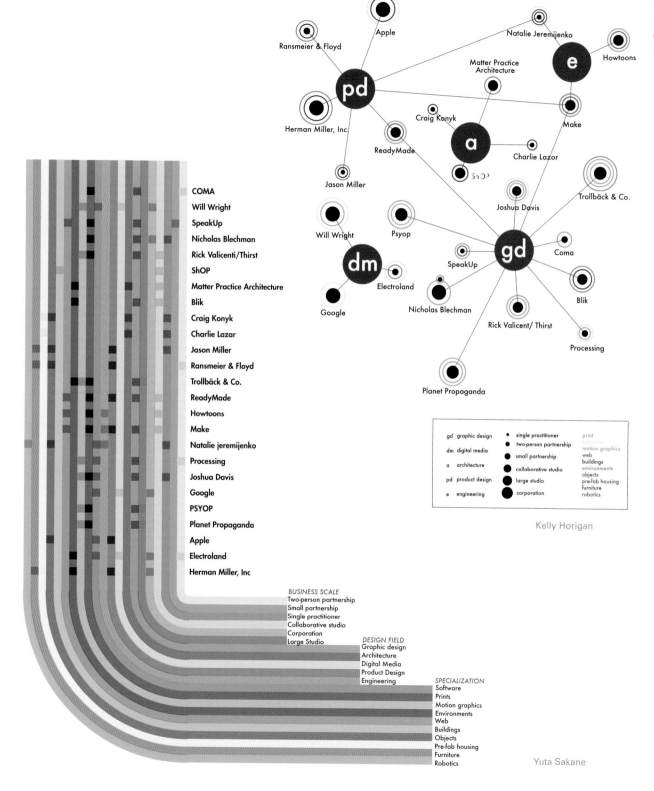

COMA
Will Wright
SpeakUp
Nicholas Blechman
Rick Valicenti/Thirst
ShOP
Matter Practice Architecture
Blik
Craig Konyk
Charlie Lazar
Jason Miller
Ransmeier & Floyd
Trollbäck & Co.
ReadyMade
Howtoons
Make
Natalie jeremijenko
Processing
Joshua Davis
Google
PSYOP
Planet Propaganda
Apple
Electroland
Herman Miller, Inc

gd graphic design
dm digital media
a architecture
pd product design
e engineering

● single practitioner
● two-person partnership
● small partnership
● collaborative studio
● large studio
● corporation

print
motion graphics
web
buildings
environments
objects
pre-fab housing
furniture
robotics

Kelly Horigan

BUSINESS SCALE
Two-person partnership
Small partnership
Single practitioner
Collaborative studio
Corporation
Large Studio

DESIGN FIELD
Graphic design
Architecture
Digital Media
Product Design
Engineering

SPECIALIZATION
Software
Prints
Motion graphics
Environments
Web
Buildings
Objects
Pre-fab housing
Furniture
Robotics

Yuta Sakane

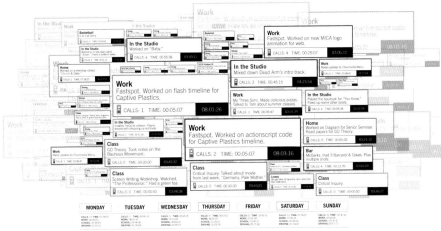

A glimpse into the life of Yianni Mathioudakis

Biodiagram This project asks designers to represent one facet of their lives according to a clear conceptual and visual framework. Form, color, and configuration must grow out of the hierarchy and nature of the content. Advanced Graphic Design. Jennifer Cole Phillips, faculty.

Overworked This diagram reflects the harried schedule of a self-supporting college student, showing his daily routines and errands. Yianni Mathioudakis.

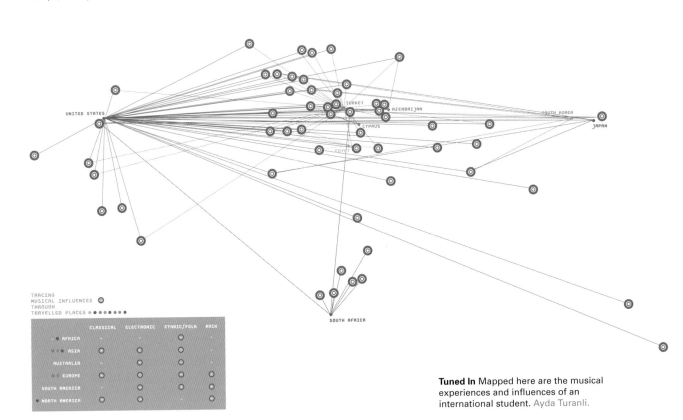

Tuned In Mapped here are the musical experiences and influences of an international student. Ayda Turanli.

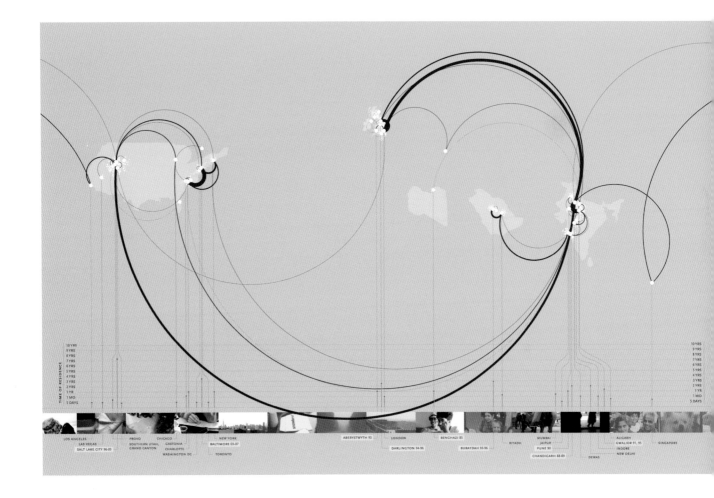

Cosmopolitan This diagram charts the
number of days, months, and years a
designer spent residing in places around
the globe, illuminated with photographic,
typographic, and diagrammatic details.
Meghana Khandekar.

Work History This circular diagram catalogs a designer's employment history by time and location. Kim Bentley, MFA Studio.

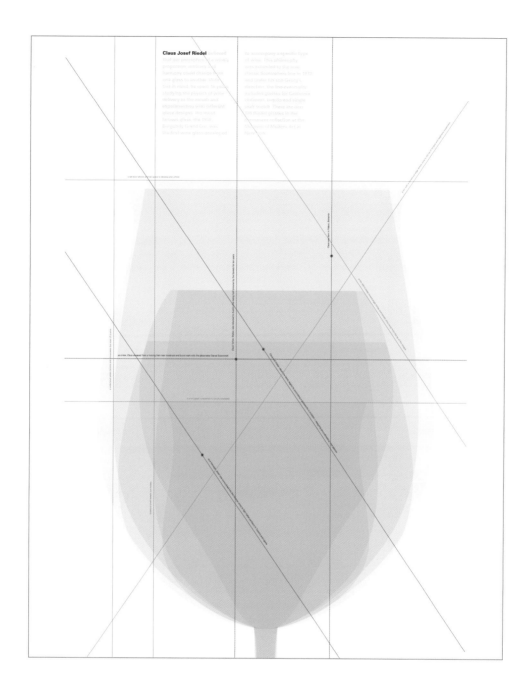

Crystal Clear Claus Josef Riedel was a
pioneering designer of wine glasses.
This poster illustrates Riedel's life work,
using transparent layers to represent
different shapes of stemware. Gregory May,
MFA Studio. Alicia Cheng, visiting faculty.

Underground Networks Created for the *New York Times Magazine* by media designer Lisa Strausfeld, this diagram visualizes complex relationships surrounding worldwide terrorist groups.

Produced using the computer language Processing, Strausfeld's diagram conveys the maddening difficulty involved in keeping track of countless potential links and dangers. Lisa Strausfeld, Pentagram.

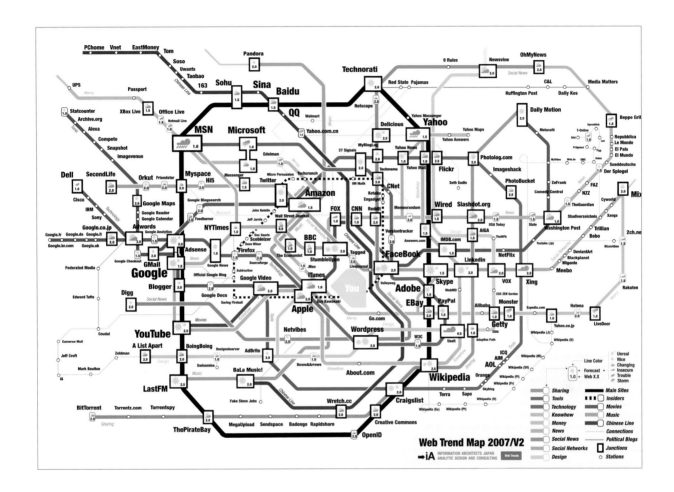

Charting Trends This seductive map selects and situates the world's two hundred most popular websites and classifies them according to categories such as design, music, moneymaking, and much more. The graphic is reminiscent of the subway map used in Tokyo, where this piece was designed. Information Architects.

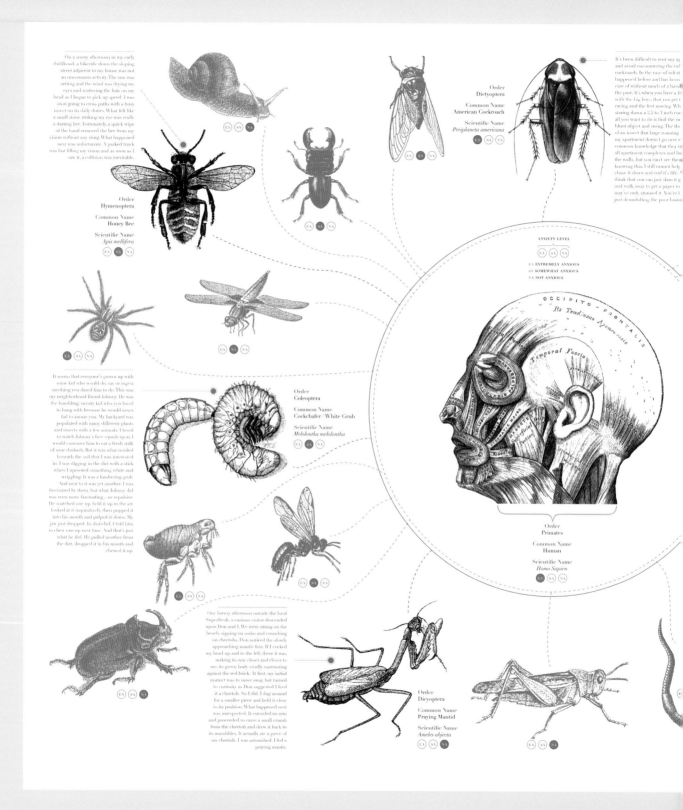

Order Dictyoptera
Common Name American Cockroach
Scientific Name *Periplaneta americana*

Order Hymenoptera
Common Name Honey Bee
Scientific Name *Apis mellifera*

Order Coleoptera
Common Name Cockchafer / White Grub
Scientific Name *Melolontha melolontha*

Order Primates
Common Name Human
Scientific Name *Homo Sapien*

Order Dictyoptera
Common Name Praying Mantid
Scientific Name *Ameles abjecta*

ANXIETY LEVEL
EA SA NA
EA EXTREMELY ANXIOUS
SA SOMEWHAT ANXIOUS
NA NOT ANXIOUS

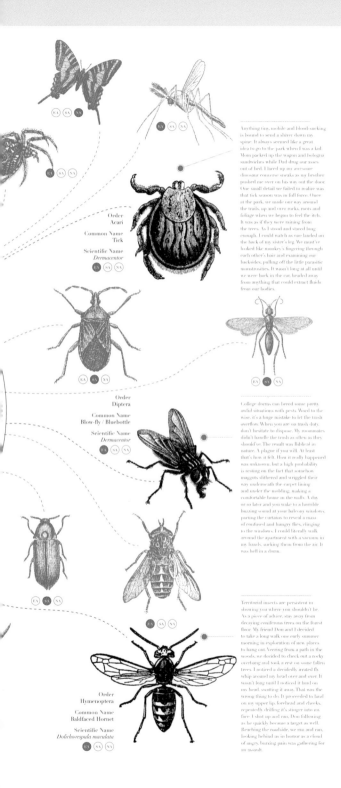

Order
Acari

Common Name
Tick

Scientific Name
Dermacentor

Order
Diptera

Common Name
Blow-fly / Bluebottle

Scientific Name
Dermacentor

Order
Hymenoptera

Common Name
Baldfaced Hornet

Scientific Name
Dolichovespula maculata

Diagramming Editorial Content
Contemporary magazine design often breaks up content, dispersing elements across the page and integrating words and images to create engaging, nonlinear experiences for readers. Principles of diagramming and mapping are thus used to organize narrative in a spatial way. Information graphics typically combine visual and verbal information, requiring mastery of both typography and composition. The literate human mind has no difficulty switching between seeing and reading.

Insect Phobia This map studies the designer's fear of various insects. The bugs with the most potent negative associations are denoted in black; lesser ones are green. An additional system calls out degrees of fear with circled letters, from extremely anxious (EA) to somewhat anxious (SA) and not anxious (NA). Memorable insect stories are recounted via warm, well-written narratives.
Jacob Lockard, Advanced Graphic Design.
Jennifer Cole Phillips, faculty.

THE
SORDID
UNDERBELLY
OF ONE GIRL'S
FILTHY
APARTMENT

A TRAGIC TALE TOLD IN 4 PARTS
13 SECTIONS, 8 SUBSECTIONS, & 1 SUBSET

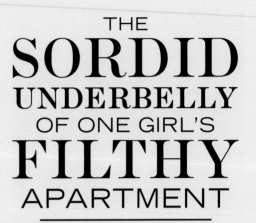

UNDER THE BATHROOM SINK:
2 bobby pins
1 ponytail elastic
1 cottonball
1 #2 pencil
1 cotton swab
$.06

UNDER THE NIGHTSTAND:
1 pair of down slippers
1 CD walkman
1 fuzzy pink knit hat
1 drimmel tool, with
   sander attachment
1 cough drop
3 dust bunnies
$.35

UNDER THE DRESSER:
1 pair of ugly tall black boots
1 pair of pretty tall brown boots
1 cordless phone
1 box of old photos - - - - - -
3 ponytail elastics
2 straw wrappers
1 dead leaf
1 dead beetle
$.51

12 BLACK-AND-WHITE FAMILY PHOTOS
20 FROM MY TRIP TO IRELAND
15 FROM MY FIRST 5 YEARS IN NYC
5 OF ME AND MY BROTHER AS KIDS
10 FROM MY CHUBBY YEARS

UNDER THE BED:
1 air mattress pump
2 flat air mattresses
2 glass bead garlands
1 pair of dark green wellies
1 coffee-stained issue of *Vogue*
1 storage bin of winter clothing - - - -
1 leopard-print slipper
1 holey sock
1 tube of cherry lip gloss
1 dead cricket
5 dust bunnies
$1.13

1 PAIR OF CORDUROYS
3 HEAVY SWEATERS
3 LONG-SLEEVE T-SHIRTS
2 PAIRS OF THERMAL UNDIES
8 PAIRS OF WOOL KNEE SOCKS
3 PAIRS OF GRAY KNIT TIGHTS

BEHIND THE BED:
2 rolling suitcases
1 military issue
   sleeping bag
1 box of tax records
3 argyle socks
1 black bikini
1 large beach towel
1 dusty cough drop
$.67

UNDER THE BOOKCASE:
1 paperback of *Jane Eyre*
3 tangled extension cords
1 pair of unflattering sunglasses
$.87

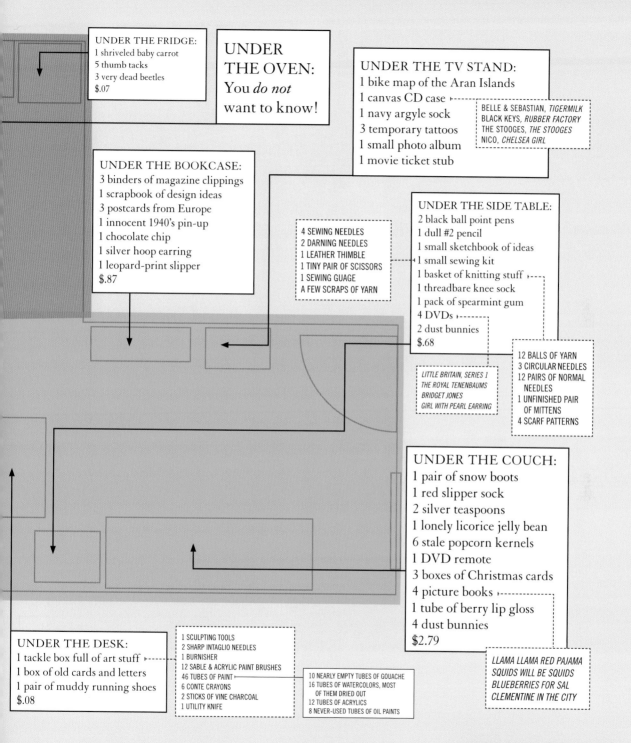

UNDER THE FRIDGE:
1 shriveled baby carrot
5 thumb tacks
3 very dead beetles
$.07

UNDER THE OVEN: You *do not* want to know!

UNDER THE TV STAND:
1 bike map of the Aran Islands
1 canvas CD case
1 navy argyle sock
3 temporary tattoos
1 small photo album
1 movie ticket stub

BELLE & SEBASTIAN, *TIGERMILK*
BLACK KEYS, *RUBBER FACTORY*
THE STOOGES, *THE STOOGES*
NICO, *CHELSEA GIRL*

UNDER THE BOOKCASE:
3 binders of magazine clippings
1 scrapbook of design ideas
3 postcards from Europe
1 innocent 1940's pin-up
1 chocolate chip
1 silver hoop earring
1 leopard-print slipper
$.87

4 SEWING NEEDLES
2 DARNING NEEDLES
1 LEATHER THIMBLE
1 TINY PAIR OF SCISSORS
1 SEWING GUAGE
A FEW SCRAPS OF YARN

UNDER THE SIDE TABLE:
2 black ball point pens
1 dull #2 pencil
1 small sketchbook of ideas
1 small sewing kit
1 basket of knitting stuff
1 threadbare knee sock
1 pack of spearmint gum
4 DVDs
2 dust bunnies
$.68

12 BALLS OF YARN
3 CIRCULAR NEEDLES
12 PAIRS OF NORMAL
    NEEDLES
1 UNFINISHED PAIR
    OF MITTENS
4 SCARF PATTERNS

LITTLE BRITAIN, SERIES 1
THE ROYAL TENENBAUMS
BRIDGET JONES
GIRL WITH PEARL EARRING

UNDER THE COUCH:
1 pair of snow boots
1 red slipper sock
2 silver teaspoons
1 lonely licorice jelly bean
6 stale popcorn kernels
1 DVD remote
3 boxes of Christmas cards
4 picture books
1 tube of berry lip gloss
4 dust bunnies
$2.79

UNDER THE DESK:
1 tackle box full of art stuff
1 box of old cards and letters
1 pair of muddy running shoes
$.08

1 SCULPTING TOOLS
2 SHARP INTAGLIO NEEDLES
1 BURNISHER
12 SABLE & ACRYLIC PAINT BRUSHES
46 TUBES OF PAINT
6 CONTE CRAYONS
2 STICKS OF VINE CHARCOAL
1 UTILITY KNIFE

10 NEARLY EMPTY TUBES OF GOUACHE
16 TUBES OF WATERCOLORS, MOST
    OF THEM DRIED OUT
12 TUBES OF ACRYLICS
8 NEVER-USED TUBES OF OIL PAINTS

LLAMA LLAMA RED PAJAMA
SQUIDS WILL BE SQUIDS
BLUEBERRIES FOR SAL
CLEMENTINE IN THE CITY

List Mania This clever editorial layout recounts every object found underneath the furniture in a designer's apartment. Elements are keyed to locations in the apartment. Kelley McIntyre, MFA Studio.

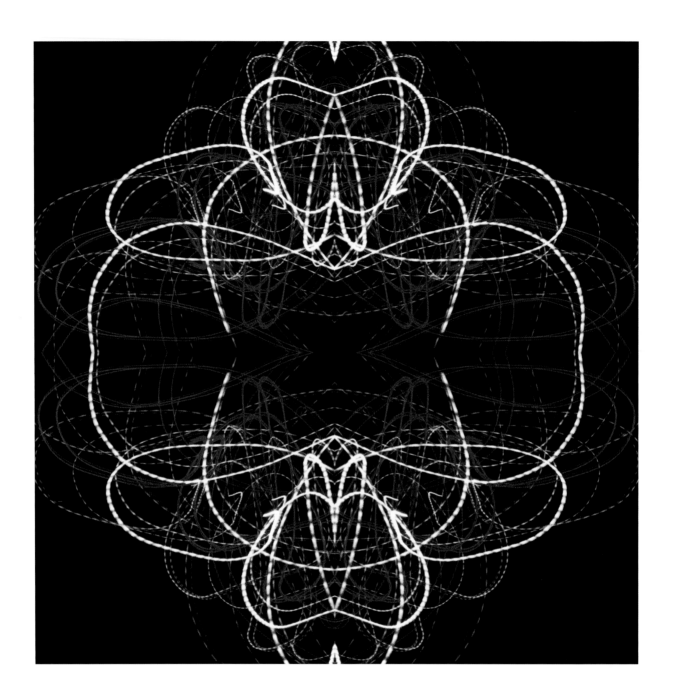

Time and Motion

Every drawing can be understood as a motion study
since it is **a path of motion** recorded by graphic means.

László Moholy-Nagy

Time and motion are closely related principles. Any word or image that moves functions both spatially and temporally. Motion is a kind of change, and change takes place in time. Motion can be implied as well as literal, however. Artists have long sought ways to represent the movement of bodies and the passage of time within the realm of static, two-dimensional space. Time and motion are considerations for all design work, from a multipage printed book, whose pages follow each other in time, to animations for film and television, which have literal duration.

Any still image has implied motion (or implied stasis), while motion graphics share compositional principles with print. Designers today routinely work in time-based media as well as print, and a design campaign often must function across multiple media simultaneously.

Animation encompasses diverse modes of visible change, including the literal movement of elements that fly on or off the screen as well as changes in scale, transparency, color, layer, and more. These alternative modes of change are especially useful for designing animated text on the web, where gratuitous movement can be more distracting than pleasing or informative.

It can be useful to think about the screen as an active, changing surface as well as a neutral stage or support onto which characters rush on and off. Thus a fixed field of dots, for example, can light up sequentially to spell out a message, or objects can become visible or invisible as the background behind them changes color or transparency. A word or design element can stay still while the environment around it changes.

Film is a visual art. Designers of motion graphics must think both like painters and typographers and like animators and filmmakers. A motion sequence is developed through a series of storyboards, which convey the main phases and movements of an animation. A style frame serves to establish the visual elements of a project, such as its colors, typefaces, illustrative components, and more. Such frames must be designed with the same attentiveness to composition, scale, color, and other principles as any work of design. In addition, the motion designer thinks about how all these components will change and interact with each other over time.

This chapter introduces some basic principles for conveying temporal change and motion, both in still and time-based media.

Long Exposure Photography A camera can capture a path of lights moving over time. The oscillations of AC currents are not visible to the eye, but, when recorded through a camera lens, the oscillations create a dashed line. DC currents generate smooth lines. Here, a single long-exposure photograph has been repeated and rotated to create a larger visual shape. Sarah Joy Jordahl Verville, MFA Studio.

Eruption of Form These shapes as well as their explosive arrangement suggest movement and change. Sasha Funk, Graphic Design I. Zvezdana Rogic, faculty.

Implied Motion

Graphic designers use numerous techniques to suggest change and movement on the printed page. Diagonal compositions evoke motion, while rectilinear arrangements appear static. Cropping a shape can suggest motion, as does a sinuous line or a pointed, triangular shape.

Static A centered object sitting parallel to the edges of the frame appears stable and unmoving.

Diagonal An object placed on a diagonal appears dynamic.

Cropped An object that is partly cut off appears to be moving into or out of the frame.

Point the Way The shape of an arrow indicates movement. Robert Ferrell and Geoff Hanssler, Digital Imaging. Nancy Froehlich, faculty.

Moment in Time A skilled photographer can capture a moving object at a dramatic instant. Steve Sheets, Digital Imaging. Nancy Froehlich, faculty.

Restless Line These scratchy, sketchy lines contrast with the static letterforms they describe. The letters were drawn with Processing code. Ahn Yeohyun, MFA Studio.

Dimensional Line The dimensionality of these curving lines gives them movement in depth. The letters were manipulated in Adobe Illustrator. Ryan Gladhill, MFA Studio.

Egg Drop Bryan McDonough

Sequential Time Showing images in a row is an accepted way to represent time or movement on a two-dimensional surface. Drawings or photographs become like words in a sentence, linked together to tell a story. The designs shown here use cropping, sequence, and placement to suggest time and movement. Digital Imaging. Nancy Froehlich, faculty.

Cat Walk Sam Trapkin

Here is the Mark Morris Dance Group, captured rehearsing *Mozart Dances* at the light-filled Mark Morris Dance Center in Brooklyn, just before the work's premiere at the Mozart Festival last August.

Completed just before the choreographer's 50th birthday,

It seems to take place in spring, in abundant happiness, and is chock full of brilliant devices for entrances and exits.

Connecting Time and Space In these layouts for a photo essay documenting a piece by choreographer Mark Morris, the floor line becomes a point of connection, bringing together numerous shots taken over time. Abbott Miller and Kristen Spilman, Pentagram. *2wice* magazine. Photography: Katherine Wolkoff.

Jaime Bennati

Implied Time and Motion An effective logotype can be applied to anything from a tiny business card to a large-scale architectural sign to a computer screen or digital projection. The logotypes shown here use a variety of graphic strategies to imply motion.

In this project, designers created a graphic identity for a conference about contemporary media art and theory called "Loop." Each solution explores the concept of the loop as a continuous, repeating sequence. The designers applied each logo to a banner in an architectural setting and to a screen-based looping animation. (Photoshop was used to simulate the installation of the banners in a real physical space.)

Lindsay Orlowski

Loop Logo Numerous techniques are used in these studies of the word "loop" to imply movement and repetition. Some designs suggest the duration of the design process itself by exposing the interface or by drawing the logo with an endless, looping line. Above, transparency is used to create an onion-skin effect; cropping the logo on the banner further implies movement. Graphic Design II. Ellen Lupton, faculty.

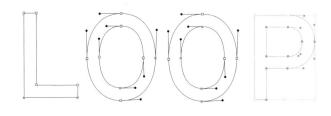

May Yang
Sueyun Choi
Lauretta Dolch

Alexandra Matzner
Lindsay Orlowski
Yuta Sakane

Key Frames Depicted here are important moments within a dancer's continuous leap. Sarah Joy Jordahl Verville, MFA Studio.

Animation Basics

Like film and other "motion pictures," animation uses sequences of still images to create the optical illusion of movement. The brain retains images for a split-second longer than the images are actually before us, resulting in the illusion of movement when numerous images appear in rapid succession. This phenomenon is called "persistence of vision." As images appear to move and come alive, the illusion is powerful and fascinating. Images for animation can be created via software, photography, and drawing.

The smallest unit of animation is the frame, a single still image. In the technique of frame-by-frame animation, a series of still images are drawn or digitally created. These still images differ from frame to frame by successive deviations in scale, orientation, color, shape, layer, and/or transparency.

In producing animation, the most important frames, called "key frames," are the fixed states that a lead designer draws or creates. In both hand-drawn and digital animation, these key frames are normally the first and last frames of each short sequence of action, indicating the start and conclusion of one or more important changes in movement. For example, the key animator may create the frame of a person about to do a cartwheel and another key frame of that same person landing at the completion of the cartwheel. Assistant artists, known as "inbetweeners," then fill in the gap by drawing the missing in-between frames, which are called "tweens." The tweens can also be generated automatically by digital animation software, which automates the time-consuming production process while making a smooth transition over time between the key frames. The process of developing these in-between frames is called "tweening."

Some professional designers and animators prefer drawing all their images using the frame-by-frame animation process, rather than by automated tweening, because it provides cleaner edges, better quality of motion, more accurate details, and greater control of subtle elements such as facial expressions. However, frame-by-frame animation is more time-consuming to produce than computer-generated motion and can result in inconsistent images. Computer-generated tweening can cause jerky lines and unwanted shadows, but it has several advantages as well. The computer's memory can provide access to databases that store previously rendered people, landscapes, buildings, and other objects, and these renderings can be used repeatedly, saving time and production costs. In addition, with computer-generated frames designers can easily adjust such variables as timing, orientation, color, layering, and scale.

In general, typography and abstract graphic elements are easily animated via automatic tweening, as compared to facial expressions or complex bodily movements.

Research and writing assistance: Sarah Joy Jordahl Verville

Composite Time and Motion Nine frames
are compressed into one image. Color moves
from warm to cool, and layers accumulate
from back to front, depicting change over
time. The assets of animation are thus used
here to compose a still image. Sarah Joy
Jordahl Verville, MFA Studio.

Change in Position Every object on a two-dimensional surface has a pair of x/y coordinates. Changing the coordinates moves the object. (3-D animation includes the z axis.) In this sequence, the object's x position is changing, while the y position is fixed, yielding a horizontal movement.

Change Over Time

All animation consists of change over time. The most obvious form of change consists of an element moving around on the screen—the Road Runner approach. The Road Runner can "walk" onto the screen like a character in a play, or it can appear there suddenly as in a cut in a film.

Changing the position of an object is just one way to make it change. Other modes of change include shifting its scale, color, shape, and transparency. By altering the degree of change and the speed with which the change takes place, the animator produces different qualities of movement. Complex and subtle behaviors are created by using different modes of change simultaneously. For example, an object can fade slowly onto the screen (changing transparency) while also getting bigger (changing in scale).

Change in Rotation Continuously altering the angle of an object creates the appearance of spinning, shaking, and other behaviors.

Change in Scale Making an object larger or smaller creates the impression of it moving backward or forward in space. Here, the object is not moving (changing its position); only its size is changing.

Change in Shape Letting a line wander can produce all types of shapes: abstract, amorphous, representational.

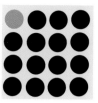 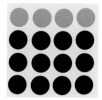 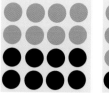

Change in Color Like a theater marquee that creates the appearance of movement by sequentially turning light bulbs on and off, color animation creates motion by sequentially illuminating or changing the color of predefined areas or objects.

Here, a wave of color appears to pass over a field of static objects. Countless variations are possible.

 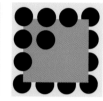 

Change in Depth Many image-editing programs allow the designer to divide an image into layers, which are comparable to the sheets of transparent acetate used in traditional cell animation.

Layers can be duplicated, deleted, altered to support new image elements, merged into a single image, and hidden. Here, objects on back layers gradually move forward.

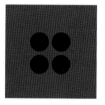 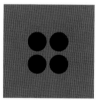 

Change in Transparency Animators alter the transparency of an image to give it the appearance of fading in or out of view. Here, the top layer gradually becomes more transparent, revealing an image behind it.

Multiple Modes of Change Most animations combine several modes of change at once.

This sequence incorporates changes in position, scale, color, and transparency.

Change in Position Moving text around the screen is the most basic means of animating type. Commonly, type enters from the right side of the screen and moves left to support the normal direction of reading. Ticker or leader text also tends to move in this direction.

Animating Type

In film and television and on the web, text is often in motion. Animating type is like animating other graphic elements, but the designer must pay special attention to legibility and reading order.

   The most elementary technique is to shift the position of a word so that it appears to move around like a character or other object. Animated words do not have to literally move, however: they can fade in or fade out; they can flicker on or off the screen letter by letter; or they can change scale, color, layer, and so on.

   When animating text, the designer adjusts the timing to make sure the words change slowly enough to be legible, but not so slowly that they become a drag to read. Context also is important. A constantly changing logo in a web banner, for example, will quickly become irritating, whereas sudden and constant motion in the title sequence of a film can help set the tone for the action to come.

Change in Color In the sequence shown here, the type itself is static, but a color change moves across the text letter by letter. Endless variations of this basic kind of change are possible.

Change in Transparency White type appears gradually on screen by gradually becoming opaque.

Multiple Modes of Change Many animations combine several techniques at once.

This sequence features change in position, scale, and transparency.

Animated Typography In this animation by Peter Cho, each letter is built from pixel-like units. The individual units as well as complete letters, words, and phrases are subject to change. Elements move in three-dimensional space and they change scale, color, and transparency.

All these complex and simultaneous changes serve to emphasize the text and make the message readable over time. Peter Cho, Imaginary Forces, 2000, for the Centers for IBM e-Business Innovation.

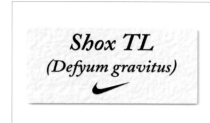

Storyboard

Since motion design can be labor-intensive, designers must plan carefully every aspect of a piece before production begins. Once a concept is developed, the script is fleshed out with storyboard sketches and a style frame. These visual tools are essential for designing commercials, online banners, television broadcast animations, and film title sequences.

   Storyboards summarize the content or key moments of an animation's events. Storyboarding also determines the flow of the storyline and suggests the major changes of action. In addition to movements, the personality, emotions, and gestures of the characters and objects are also expressed. The layout of a storyboard, similar to that of a comic strip, consists of sketches or illustrations displayed sequentially to visualize an animated or live-action piece. Notes describing camera angles, soundtrack, movement, special effects, timing, and transitions between scenes are often included.

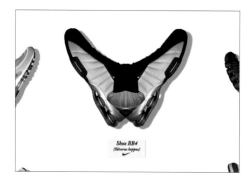

Style Frame

The ultimate look of an animation is expressed in one or more style frames, which set the aesthetic tone and formal elements. A style frame captures many of the graphic elements used throughout the piece. The typography, colors, patterns, illustrations, and photographs chosen for the project are often included.

Storyboarding and developing style frames are creative processes that allow the designer to plan and brainstorm before the animation is realized. These tools serve as guides to production and vehicles for presentation to clients. Successful style frames and storyboards are always clearly defined and easy to interpret.

Metamorphosis This animated advertisement for Nike shoes, designed by Trollbäck and Company, presents golf shoes that are mounted like butterflies in a museum frame. The shoes come to life and fly away. The meaning of the scene changes as the camera moves in and out to reveal the context.

Director: Joe Wright. Designers: Jens Mebes, Todd Neale, Justin Meredith. Creative Directors: Jakob Trollbäck and Joe Wright. Editor: Cass Vanini. Producer: Elizabeth Kiehner. Client: Nike, Ron Dumas.

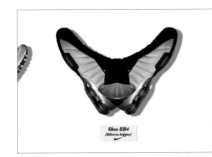

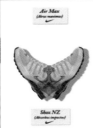

Air Max
(Aëros maximus)

Shox BB4
(Saltorus hoppus)

Shox NZ
(Hizardus impactus)

1975 LDV
(Stylus superioris)

Shox BB4
(Saltorus hoppus)

Dri-Fit Tour
(Walkum fairwayus)

Dri-Fit Tour
(Walkum fairwayus)

Dri-Fit Tour
(Walkum fairwayus)

Dri-Fit Tour
(Walkum fairwayus)

The Origin of the SP Series

A Hybrid
Athletics fused with classic golf

The new evolution in golf footwear.

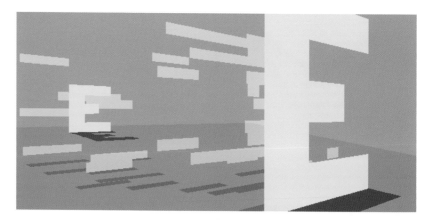

Beyond the Timeline

Interactive logos and graphics are another aspect of motion design. Rather than devising a narrative sequence with a fixed beginning and end, the interactive designer creates behaviors. These behaviors involve change over time, just like narrative animations, but they do not occur in a fixed sequence, and they are not designed using storyboards and timelines.

Interactive graphics are created with code, such as Flash ActionScript, Java, or Processing. Instead of working with the interface of a linear timeline, the designer writes functions, variables, if/then statements, and other instructions to define how the graphics will behave.

Interactive graphics need not be complex or hyperactive. Simple behaviors can delight users and enrich the experience of a digital interface. For example, an interactive logo on a webpage can wait quietly until it is touched with the user's mouse; instead of being an annoying distraction, the graphics come to life only when called upon to do so.

Letterscapes In these interactive graphics by Peter Cho, the letters dance, bounce, unravel, and otherwise transform themselves in response to mouse input. Peter Cho, 2002.

Type Me Again Simple pie shapes rotate
and repeat to create the letters of the
alphabet when users type in letters on their
keyboards. Peter Cho, 2000.

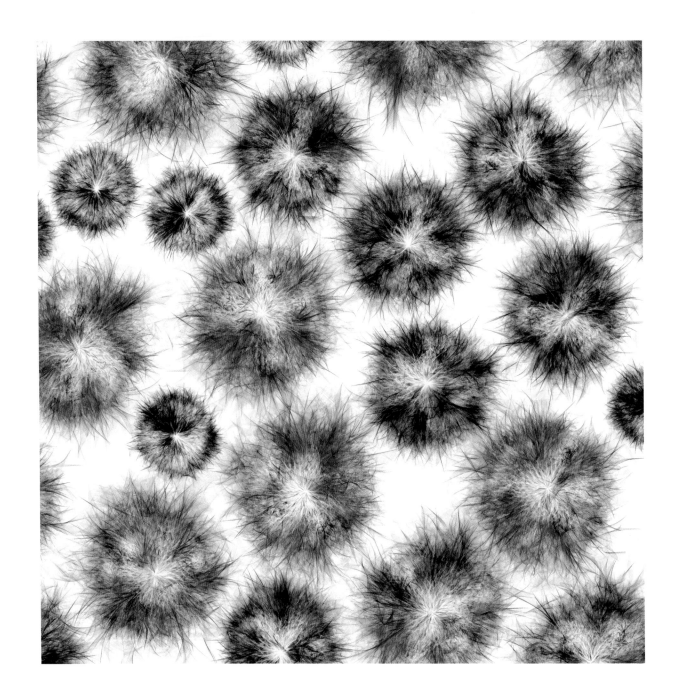

Rules and Randomness

The idea becomes a **machine** that makes the art. Sol LeWitt

Designers create rules as well as finished pieces. A magazine designer, for example, works with a grid and a typographic hierarchy that is interpreted in different ways, page after page, issue after issue. If the rules are well planned, other designers will be able to interpret them to produce their own unique and unexpected layouts. Rules create a framework for design without determining the end results.

Style sheets employed in print and web publishing (CSS) are rules for displaying the different parts of a document. By adjusting a style sheet, the designer can change the appearance of an entire book or website. Style sheets are used to reconfigure a single body of content for output in different media, from printed pages to the screen of a mobile phone.

Rules can be used to generate form as well as organize content. In the 1920s, the Bauhaus artist and designer László Moholy-Nagy created a painting by telephoning a set of instructions to a sign painter. In the 1960s, the minimalist artist Sol LeWitt created drawings based on simple instructions; the drawings could be executed on a wall or other surface anywhere in the world by following the directions. Complex webs of lines often resulted from seemingly simple verbal instructions.

Designers produce rules in computer code as well as natural language. C. E. B. Reas, who co-authored the software language Processing, creates rich digital drawings and interactive works that evolve from instructions and variables. Reas alters the outcome by changing the variables. He explains, "Sometimes I set strict rules, follow them, and then observe the results. More frequently, I begin with a core software behavior, implement it, and then observe the results. I then allow the piece to flow intuitively from there."[1] Reas and other contemporary artists are using software as a medium unto itself rather than as a tool supporting the design process.

Designing rules and instructions is an intrinsic part of the design process. Increasingly, designers are asked to create systems that other people will implement and that will change over time. This chapter looks at ways to use rule-based processes to generate unexpected visual results.

Unnatural Growth Created in Processing, this work by C. E. B. Reas resembles an organic process. The forms are created in response to rules governing the behavior of an initial set of points. The work builds over time as the program runs through its iterations. C. E. B. Reas. *Process 6 (Image 3)*, 2005 (detail).

1. C. E. B. Reas, "Process/Drawing," (Statement for the exhibition at the bitforms gallery, New York, March 4–April 2, 2005).

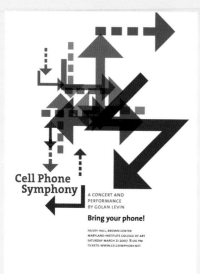

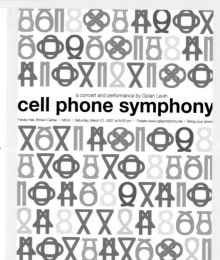

Numbers are replaced with icons from different symbol fonts. Marleen Kuijf.

Strange hieroglyphs are created by doubling and flipping each numeral. Katie Evans.

Cell Phone Symphony In the project shown here, students were given a list of phone numbers from which to generate visual imagery for a poster. The posters promote a "cell phone symphony," featuring music composed via interaction among the audience's cell phones.

Each poster suggests auditory experience as well as ideas of social and technological interaction. The students took numerous different approaches, from turning each phone number into a linear graph to using the digits to set the size and color of objects in a grid.

Designing the system is part of the creative process. The visual results have an organic quality that comes from random input to the system. The designer controls and manipulates the system itself rather than the final outcome. Graphic Design II. Ellen Lupton, faculty.

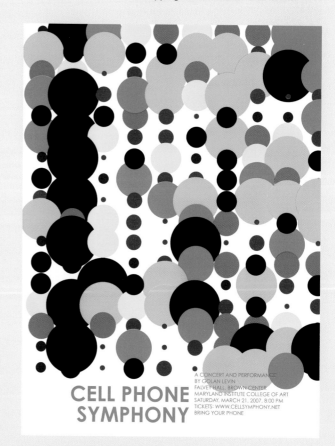

Numbers are used to set the color and size of dots on a grid. Hayley Griffin.

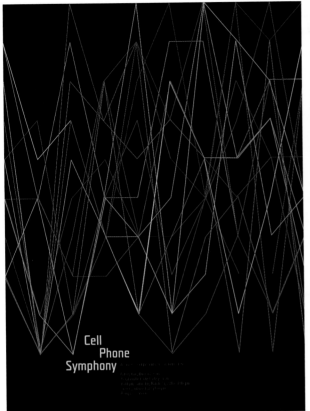

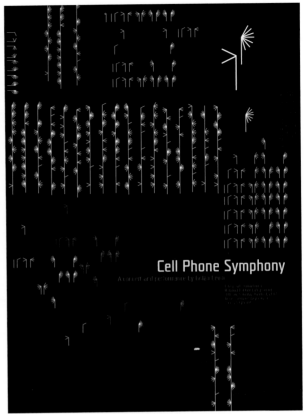

Each ten-digit number is a linear graph.
Martina Novakova.

Each phone number is a twig that sprouts marks for its digits. Martina Novakova.

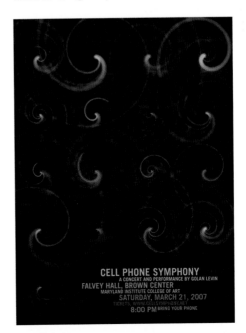

Computer code is used to create a spiraling path for each number. Jonnie Hallman.

Mechanical Drawing The drawing was made with a child's sketching toy; the lines were created by turning the dial in response to a random list of phone numbers. The hand lettering also combines order and technology with primitive, childlike techniques. Luke Williams.

Audio Waves Captured from an audio editing program, the lines represent different voices speaking a list of phone numbers. Sisi Recht.

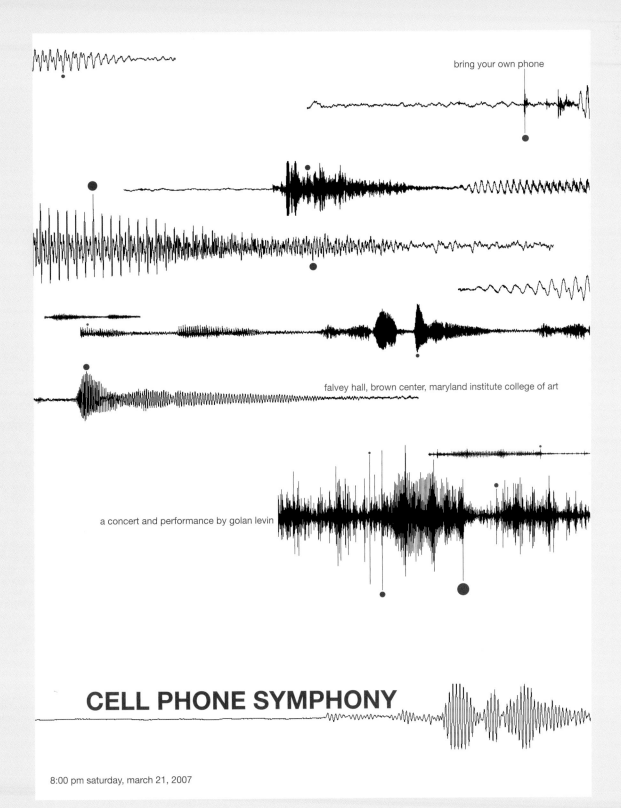

bring your own phone

falvey hall, brown center, maryland institute college of art

a concert and performance by golan levin

CELL PHONE SYMPHONY

8:00 pm saturday, march 21, 2007

Repeat and Rotate

Repeating and rotating forms are universal principles of pattern design. The designs shown here were created in the Processing software language. By altering the input to a set of digital instructions, the designer can quickly see numerous variations of a single design. Changing the typeface, type size, type alignment, color, transparency, and the number and degree of rotations yields different results.

```
for(int i=0;i<12;i++){
fill(0,0,0);
textAlign(CENTER);
pushMatrix();

rotate(PI*i/6);

text("F",0,0);
popMatrix();
}
}
```

Similar effects can be achieved by rotating and repeating characters in standard graphics programs such as Illustrator. Working in Processing or other code languages allows the designer to test and manipulate different variables while grasping the logic and mathematics behind pattern design.

Yeohyun Ahn

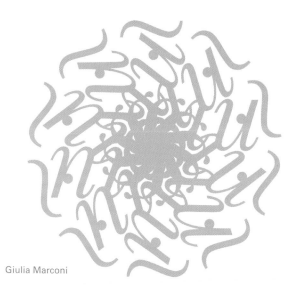

Giulia Marconi

Giulia Marconi

Rotated Letterforms A simple code structure is used to generate designs with surprising intricacy. New designs can be quickly tested by changing the variables. Graphic Design II. Ellen Lupton and Yeohyun Ahn, faculty.

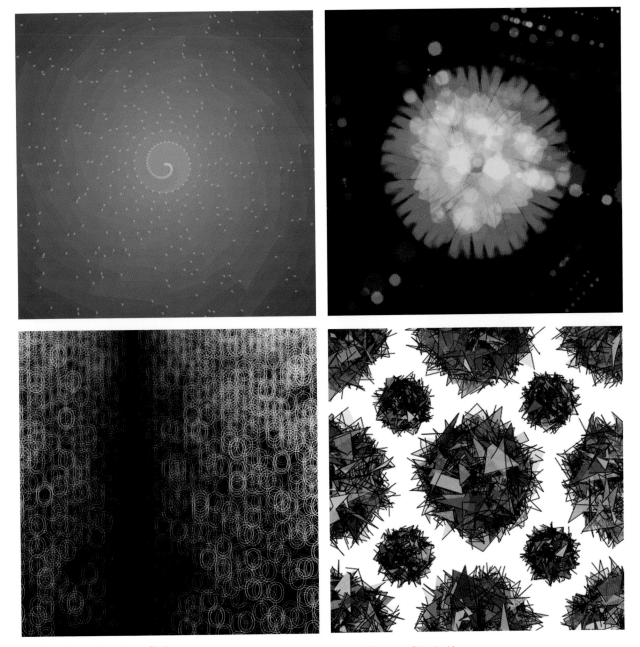

Jonnie Hallman, Shin Hyung Choi

Jessica Till, Adam Okrasinski

Repeat and Random One or two simple elements are repeated using a "for" statement. The transparency, size, or x and y coordinates are randomized to create a sense of natural motion. Graphic Design II. Ellen Lupton and Yeohyun Ahn, faculty.

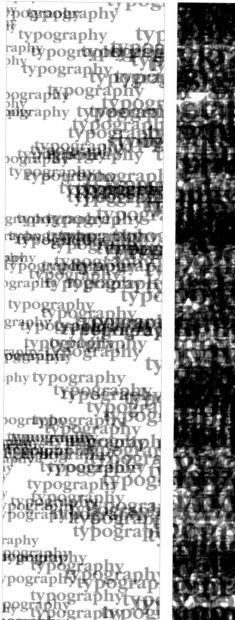

Type Swarm Here, the draw function in Processing has been used to randomly place the letter A on the screen, beginning from one starting point in the upper left hand corner of the screen. Yeohyun Ahn and Ryan Gladhill, MFA Studio.

Game of Life Using code written by Mike Davis and inspired by John Conway's Game of Life, this animation of the word "typography" uses variables with random functions, yielding a rich, soft pattern. Yeohyun Ahn and Viviana Cordova, MFA Studio.

Center of Gravity These typographic studies
use numerous Bézier curves to describe the
edges of letterforms. Each line originates
from the center and connects to points along
the outline of the letters. The center point
and the curves can be changed to yield
different results. Yeohyun Ahn, MFA Studio.

Nature and Software This naturalistic tree is created by software interacting with audio input from a user. Without sound the program only generates branches, but when sound is input, the tree grows leaves. The color of the leaves corresponds with the time of day. The tree grows green leaves during the day, and black leaves at night.

The piece was created using Processing with an external library, Sonia, which provides real-time frequency analysis of the microphone input. The designer created a program that generates fractals, referencing the L-system algorithm, programmed by Jer Thorp. Yeohyun Ahn, Physical Interface Design. Ryan McCabe, faculty.

Tree = {"FF-[-F+F+F-]+[+F-F-F+]:90",
"++:5", "--:5"};

Bibliography

Basics

Arnheim, Rudolf. *Visual Thinking.* Berkeley: University of California Press, 1969.

Arnston, Amy. *Graphic Design Basics.* New York: Holt Rinehart and Winston, 1988.

Booth-Clibborn, Edward, and Daniele Baroni. *The Language of Graphics.* New York: Harry N. Abrams, 1979.

Carter, Rob, Ben Day, and Phillip Meggs. *Typographic Design: Form and Communication.* New York: Wiley, 2002. First published 1985.

Dondis, Donis. *A Primer of Visual Literacy.* Cambridge, MA: MIT Press, 1973.

Garland, Ken. *Graphics Handbook.* New York: Reinhold, 1966.

Graham, Lisa. *Basics of Design: Layout and Typography for Beginners.* Florence, KY: Thomson Delmar Learning, 2001.

Grear, Malcolm. *Inside/Outside: From the Basics to the Practice of Design.* New York: AIGA and New Riders, 2006.

Hofmann, Armin. *Graphic Design Manual: Principles and Practice.* New York: Reinhold, 1966.

Kandinsky, Wassily. *Point and Line to Plane.* New York: Dover, 1979.

Klee, Paul. *Pedagogical Sketchbook.* London: Faber and Faber, 1953.

Koren, Leonard, and R. Wippo Meckler. *The Graphic Design Cookbook: Mix and Match Recipes for Faster, Better Layouts.* San Francisco: Chronicle Books, 2001.

Krause, Jim. *Layout Index.* Cincinnati, OH: North Light Books, 2001.

Landa, Robin. *Graphic Design Solutions.* Florence, KY: OnWord Press, 2000.

Leborg, Christian. *Visual Grammar.* New York: Princeton Architectural Press, 2006.

Newark, Quentin. *What is Graphic Design?* East Sussex, UK: RotoVision, 2002.

Rand, Paul. *Paul Rand: A Designer's Art.* New Haven: Yale University Press, 1985.

Resnick, Elizabeth. *Design for Communication: Conceptual Graphic Design Basics.* New York: Wiley, 2003.

Rüegg, Ruedi. *Basic Typography: Design with Letters.* New York: Van Nostrand Reinhold, 1989.

Skolos, Nancy, and Thomas Wedell. *Type, Image, Message: A Graphic Design Layout Workshop.* Gloucester, MA: Rockport Publishers, 2006.

White, Alex. *The Elements of Graphic Design: Space, Unity, Page Architecture, and Type.* New York: Allworth Press, 2002.

Wilde, Richard, and Judith Wilde. *Visual Literacy: A Conceptual Approach to Graphic Problem-Solving.* New York: Watson-Guptill, 2005.

Williams, Robin. *The Non-Designer's Design Book.* Berkeley, CA: Peachpit Press, 2003.

Code

Dawes, Brendan. *Analog In, Digital Out: Brendan Dawes on Interaction Design.* Berkeley, CA: New Riders Press, 2006.

Gerstner, Karl. *Designing Programmes.* Zurich: ABC Verlag, 1963.

Maeda, John. *Creative Code.* London: Thames and Hudson, 2004.

Reas, Casey, Ben Fry, and John Maeda. *Processing: A Programming Handbook for Visual Designers and Artist.* Cambridge, MA: MIT Press, 2007.

Reas, C. E. B. *Process/Drawing.* Berlin: DAM, 2005.

Color

AdamsMorioka and Terry Stone. *Color Design Workbook: A Real-World Guide to Using Color in Graphic Design.* Gloucester, MA: Rockport Press, 2006.

Albers, Josef. *Interaction of Color.* New Haven: Yale University Press, 2006. First published 1963.

Krause, Jim. *Color Index.* Cincinnati: How Design Books, 2002.

Diagram

Bhaskaran, Lakshmi. *Size Matters: Effective Graphic Design for Large Amounts of Information.* Mies, Switzerland: RotoVision, 2004.

Tufte, Edward R. *Beautiful Evidence.* Cheshire, CT: Graphics Press, 2006.

———. *Envisioning Information.* Cheshire, CT: Graphics Press, 1990.

Grid

Bosshard, Hans Rudolf. *Der Typografische Raster/The Typographic Grid.* Sulgen, Switzerland: Verlag Niggli, 2000.

Elam, Kimberly. *Geometry of Design.* New York: Princeton Architectural Press, 2001.

———. *Grid Systems: Principles of Organizing Type.* New York: Princeton Architectural Press, 2005.

Jute, André. *Grids: The Structure of Graphic Design.* Mies, Switzerland: RotoVision, 1996.

Müller-Brockmann, Josef. *Grid Systems in Graphic Design.* Santa Monica, CA: RAM Publications, 1996. First published 1961.

Samara, Timothy. *Making and Breaking the Grid: A Graphic Design Layout Workshop.* Gloucester, MA: Rockport Publishers, 2002.

History and Theory

Alexander, Christopher. "The City is Not a Tree." In *Architecture Culture, 1943–1968: A Documentary Anthology*, edited by Joan Ockman. New York: Rizzoli, 1993, 379–88.

Arnheim, Rudolf. *Art and Visual Perception.* Berkeley: University of California Press, 1974.

Derrida, Jacques. *The Truth in Painting.* Translated by Geoff Bennington and Ian McCleod. Chicago: University of Chicago Press, 1987.

Fish, Stanley. "Devoid of Content." *New York Times.* May 31, 2005, Op-Ed page.

Franciscono, Marcel. *Walter Gropius and the Creation of the Bauhaus.* Urbana: University of Illinois Press, 1971.

Galloway, Alexander, and Eugene Thacker. "Protocol, Control and Networks." *Grey Room* 12 (2004): 6–29.

Itten, Johannes. *Design and Form: The Basic Course at the Bauhaus and Later.* New York: Van Nostrand Reinhold, 1975.

Johnson, Steven. *Everything Bad Is Good for You: How Today's Popular Culture is Actually Making Us Smarter.* New York: Penguin, 2005.

Kepes, Gyorgy. *Language of Vision.* Chicago: Paul Theobold, 1947.

Lupton, Ellen and J. Abbott Miller. *Design Writing Research: Writing on Graphic Design.* London: Phaidon, 1999.

Manovich, Lev. "Generation Flash." http://www.manovich.net (accessed May 10, 2006).

———. *The Language of New Media.* Cambridge, MA: MIT Press, 2001.

Margolin, Victor. *The Struggle for Utopia: Rodchenko, Lissitzky, Moholy-Nagy, 1917–1946.* Chicago: University of Chicago Press, 1998.

McCoy, Katherine. "Hybridity Happens." *Emigre* 67 (2004): 38–47.

———. "The New Discourse." In *Cranbrook: The New Design Discourse*, by Katherine McCoy and Michael McCoy. New York: Rizzoli, 1990.

————. "When Designers Create Culture." *Print* LVI: III (2002): 26, 181–3.

Moholy-Nagy, László. *Vision in Motion.* Chicago: Paul Theobold, 1969. First published 1947.

Moholy-Nagy, Sibyl. *Moholy-Nagy: Experiment in Totality.* Cambridge, MA: MIT Press, 1950.

Naylor, Gillian. *The Bauhaus Reassessed.* New York: E. P. Dutton, 1985.

Rowe, Colin, and Robert Slutzky. "Transparency: Literal and Phenomenal (Part 2)." In *Architecture Culture, 1943–1968: A Documentary Anthology,* edited by Joan Ockman. New York: Rizzoli, 1993, 205–225.

Weber, Nicholas Fox. *Josef + Anni Albers: Designs for Living.* London: Merrell Publishers, 2004.

Weingart, Wolfgang. *My Way to Typography.* Baden, Switzerland: Lars Müller Publishers, 2000.

Wick, Rainer K., and Gabriele D. Grawe. *Teaching at the Bauhaus.* Ostfildern-Ruit, Germany: Hatje Cantz Publishers, 2000.

Wingler, Hans M. *The Bauhaus.* Cambridge, MA: MIT Press, 1986.

Pattern

Archibald Christie. *Traditional Methods of Pattern Designing; An Introduction to the Study of the Decorative Art.* Oxford: Clarendon Press, 1910.

Hagan, Keith. *The Complete Pattern Library.* New York: Harry N. Abrams, 2005.

Jones, Owen. *The Grammar of Ornament.* Edited by Maxine Lewis. London: DK Adult, 2001. First published 1856.

Time and Motion

Furniss, Maureen. *Art in Motion: Animation Aesthetics.* London: John Libbey, 1998.

Williams, Richard. *The Animator's Survival Kit: A Manual of Methods, Principles, and Formulas for Classical, Computer, Games, Stop Motion and Internet Animators.* London: Faber and Faber, 2001.

Woolman, Matt, and Jeff Bellantoni. *Moving Type: Designing for Time and Space.* Mies, Switzerland: RotoVision, 2000.

Typography

Baines, Phil, and Andrew Haslam. *Type and Typography.* New York: Watson-Guptill Publications, 2002.

Bringhurst, Robert. *The Elements of Typographic Style.* Vancouver: Hartley and Marks, 1997.

Carter, Rob, Ben Day, and Philip Meggs. *Typographic Design: Form and Communication.* New York: Van Nostrand Reinhold, 1993.

Elam, Kimberly. *Typographic Systems.* New York: Princeton Architectural Press, 2007.

French, Nigel. *InDesign Type.* Berkeley, CA: Adobe Press, 2006.

Kane, John. *A Type Primer.* London: Laurence King, 2002.

Kunz, Willi. *Typography: Formation and Transformation.* Sulgen, Switzerland: Verlag Niggli, 2003.

————. *Typography: Macro- and Microaesthetics.* Sulgen, Switzerland: Verlag Niggli, 2004.

Lupton, Ellen. *Thinking with Type: A Critical Guide for Designers, Writers, Editors, and Students.* New York: Princeton Architectural Press, 2004.

Ruder, Emil. *Typography.* New York: Hastings House, 1971.

Spiekermann, Erik, and E. M. Ginger. *Stop Stealing Sheep and Find Out How Type Works.* Mountain View, CA: Adobe Press, 1993.

Index

Student Contributors

Colophon

Book Typography
Univers family, designed by Adrian Frutiger, 1957

Cover Typography
Knockout, designed by Jonathan Hoefler, 1993–97